JAKOB + MACFARLANE

JAKOB + MACFARLANE

Published in Australia in 2006 by
The Images Publishing Group Pty Ltd
ABN 89 059 734 431
6 Bastow Place, Mulgrave, Victoria 3170, Australia
Tel: +61 3 9561 5544 Fax: +61 3 9561 4860
books@images.com.au
www.imagespublishing.com

Copyright © The Images Publishing Group Pty Ltd 2006
The Images Publishing Group Reference Number: 626

National Library of Australia Cataloguing-in-Publication entry:

Jakob & MacFarlane.

Bibliography.

ISBN 1 920744 83 5.

1. Jakob & MacFarlane (Firm). 2. Architectural firms – France – Paris – History. 3. Architecture,
Modern – 20th century. 4. Architecture, Modern – 21st century.

I. Pavlovits, Daniel. II. Jakob & MacFarlane (Firm). III. Title : Jakob and MacFarlane.
(Series: Neo Architecture).

720.944361

Edited by Robyn Beaver

Designed by The Graphic Image Studio Pty Ltd, Mulgrave, Australia
www.tgis.com.au

Digital production by Splitting Image Colour Studio Pty Ltd, Australia
Printed by Everbest Printing Co. Ltd. in Hong Kong/China

IMAGES has included on its website a page for special notices in relation to this and our other publications.
Please visit www.imagespublishing.com

CONTENTS

This book showcases the work of Jakob+MacFarlane, a practice based in Paris, France. The firm's principals, Dominique Jakob and Brendan MacFarlane, were educated at some of the most distinguished schools of architecture: Dominique Jakob received her degree from the Ecole d'Architecture Paris-Villemin; Brendan MacFarlane graduated from the Southern California Institute of Architecture (SCi-Arch) in the United States and later went on to receive a Masters in Architecture from Harvard Graduate School of Design.

The sensibility of their work heavily engages the capture and articulation of movement, both ethereal in terms of, for instance, meteorology as in their House H project, and real in terms of the body's circulation in space, such as in their Restaurant Georges project for the Center Pompidou or their Branly Museum international competition entry. The firm's concern with movement is one of capturing and articulating vectors of force in order to articulate a dynamic sensibility in their work. This desire can be seen as a translation of the so-called zeitgeist of our time, not just in terms of articulating an essence of global communication and information technologies and their impact on our subjectivity in the twenty-first century, but also by utilising that technologically in conceiving and then creating architectural form that escapes the traditional representation of architecture as a static art. Jakob and MacFarlane achieve sophistication in their design schemes by employing high-end digital computer technology in their design process.

It should not be seen as coincidental that a French architecture firm has managed to create such distinction. The intellectual context and conception of their work can best be situated as being influenced by a post-structuralist philosophical reading of their French contemporaries in philosophy, foremost amongst them the writings and sensibility of Gilles Deleuze as expressed in his books such as *Cinema I* and *Cinema II*. A further influence from the writings of Deleuze can be seen in the way they address topological structures through

FOREWORD

applying and extrapolating Deleuze's concept of the 'fold' in their architectural solution – as discussed in Deleuze's highly influential text *The Fold – Leibniz and the Baroque*. This influence can most readily be appreciated in their Puzzle House project, designed to provide an alternative prototype to mass-produced residential housing.

The topological concerns Jakob and MacFarlane pursue in their work, together with their desire to capture and express movement, and their utilisation of the computer and digital design methods to realise these goals, position the conceptual design process of the firm at the cutting-edge of architectural practice today. However, pushing the boundaries of their profession does not stop at the conceptual. Jakob and MacFarlane equally pursue a level of excellence and attention to detail in the conception of novel fabrication methods, also realised through computer-aided methods, as can be seen in their Restaurant Georges project, for example.

Jakob+MacFarlane has been distinguished by being invited twice to represent France at the Venice Architectural Biennale, first in 2002 and then again in 2004, and has also been invited to exhibit at the inaugural Architectural Biennale in Beijing, China. The firm's work has been published and exhibited widely, and is rightly proclaimed as a highly promising collaborative, representing the best in French architecture and architectural sensibility heading into the twenty-first century.

Jakob and MacFarlane participate in competitions on a regular basis. In addition to the numerous invited competition entries, they have also executed a series of exhibition designs over the years both in France and abroad. This book showcases built architectural projects of Jakob+MacFarlane, either already completed or currently under construction, as well as theoretical and exhibition projects.

Daniel Pavlovits
Series Editor
Neo Architecture Series

Among the contemporary architects who have effectively registered this crucial paradigm shift in the architectural field stand Paris-based Dominique Jakob and Brendan MacFarlane, whose projects address the contradictory goal of opening up to events and of materialising precise functional performances. A genealogical review of their projects would clearly outline the continuity of strategies the firm has adopted from the start, and the developments that each completed work has brought. In constantly reforming and reworking a set of ideas among which topology is always present, this work has been growing over the years, representing a cumulative expertise deserving critical examination.

Their interest towards a light, porous and moving architecture can be read in each work from the early Puzzle House project of 1997 to the Renault Communication Center. In interacting with the hard logics of matter and fabrication, they find the deep induction forces driving the design process. What

remains particularly noteworthy with this practice is the degree of autonomy it maintains in respect to the common urge of being 'of its day'. If they are definitely active in contemporary culture by exploring means of making ideas with the latest conceptual tools and technologies available, their work succeeds in overcoming the avant-garde paradox, and produces instead lasting projects, conceived for today and tomorrow without losing its momentum in the turnover process presently encountered in every field of activity.

The Puzzle House stands in retrospect as a manifesto, incorporating a set of questions that will be addressed in most of the projects thereafter: the blurring of the ground-wall-sky tri-partition, the folding of surfaces, the reinterpretation of context or given conditions in a spatial proposition. For example, their rehabilitation and transformation of the Gorki Theater enabled Jakob and MacFarlane to elaborate a strategy of smooth intervention in existing

buildings, blending together specific data coming from geometry and urban landscape. The theatre, located in a suburban neighbourhood, was previously a movie theatre, which inherited uncommon proportions for such a building. The project went through a chopping of the domestic volume as a memory of the previous urban lots, and from there produced the equivalent of a binocular viewing machine, the public being thrown in a direct frontal interface with the scene.

What worked with such strength with the Beaubourg restaurant, Georges, was the acute choreographical relation installed between the Piano/Rogers masterpiece and the resultant restaurant scheme. In this masterpiece, rooted in the Archigram projects of the 1960s, Jakob+MacFarlane inscribed and built the very ideals and formal configurations that made Beaubourg possible in the first place: flexibility and supple space. If Beaubourg was a dream of the 1960s becoming real in the mid-1970s, Georges is a dream of the

INTRODUCTION

1960s that could not be built before the 1990s. The Georges restaurant unlocks the very potentials offered by the original building when it was erected in 1977: while the Centre has definitely become a piece of history, its restaurant saves it from a preservation syndrome. It is no great feat to refurbish, or rejuvenate an architecture; it is another challenge to be able to mingle intimately through its deep logic and to exacerbate it without disturbance. Again, we see here at play a powerful autonomy towards the existing, and a refined intelligence of what is at stake in the context. The Renault project (2002–04) achieves exactly such an operation and so did the competition entry for the Branly Art Museum (2000), which was in direct filiation with the experiments put into practice in the restaurant Georges. The different volumes that constitute the programme of the Museum are spread onto a flat surface so that visitors can pass seamlessly from one space to the other, transporting themselves from one culture to another civilization.

In fitting out the Florence Loewy bookshop, a parallel strategy is applied, and the project offers a never-seen answer to the usual question of the presentation of books. The curvilinear shelves blow up and fill the space, investing it with a landscape-like formation. Thanks to the 3D wood-frame grid, which also provides book storage space, one of the primary programmatic constraints of a bookshop finds its correct answer. The Loewy bookshop is about virtual skin, the structure producing the space and the skin remaining almost nowhere; the books generated the grid, the structure, to which was added the imaginary paths of the clients from the street to the books and back, as if an 'evacuation' in space was produced by the movements of the bodies. Here, the project focuses on an architecture of the 'after', an architecture conceived as the result of events and flux, revealing a system that is then put under critique. An overriding system is matched with multiple conditions and deformations equivalent to random browsing in space for books.

A remarkable feature of Jakob and MacFarlane's practice is the ability to shift smoothly from one scale of project to another with similar morphological principles, without falling into the trap of literal self-quotations or redundancy. From the Loewy Bookshop to the 100 Apartments block in Paris, one encounters a similar structural system but in each case, in a sense, 'it happens for other reasons'.

When dealing with auditoriums and theatres, programmes which became an important part of Jakob and MacFarlane's workload, the duo is interested in rethinking the space between the stage and the public. This is experienced at its best in the Fanal Theatre in Saint-Nazaire, where attention is given to the footprints and a portion of the remaining railway station façade. The 4.5-metre x 4.5-metre grid of the existing building is transformed into a floating conceptual grid at 8 metres above ground and a horizontal grid is thus established to produce a multi-boxed project generated from the existing geometric grid.

Such a box and topographic strategy is akin to the work on the mesh-land topography developed for the House H in Corsica. In the Renault Conference Center the given data was a 60-degree section, which generated shapes through folding operations. Here, the roof was the project's ignition material, whereas in Beaubourg, and also in the Branly Museum, it was the ground.

Presence, double-skin strategies, topological effects and production processes, are thus among the numerous notions with which the Jakob+MacFarlane team operate, using a subtle and profound approach inscribing their work on the international map of firms devoted to a serious research agenda.

Christian Girard

i Benjamin, Andrew, 'Time , function and alterity in architecture', in *Architectural Philosophy* (London, The Athlone Press, 2000), p. 36.

The house is organised around a patio, allowing circulation and views, and encouraging reflection and participation in family life, while the space beyond the confines of the plan of the house is public space.

On the basis of this definition of public and private, the house, associated landscaping and the access road were interpreted as pieces of a jigsaw puzzle that are assembled in so-called deformed or fractured space. The interlocking pieces of the 'puzzle', as set in the landscape of the site, offer variable composition, creating a rich series of possibilities from a limited series of components, but one that is invariably structured in relation to the connections to be made between public and private, inside and outside.

1

PUZZLE HOUSE

Project for exhibition 1997

Theoretical project

1   Section axonometric view
2   Site model – collection Pompidou Centre
3   Plan view

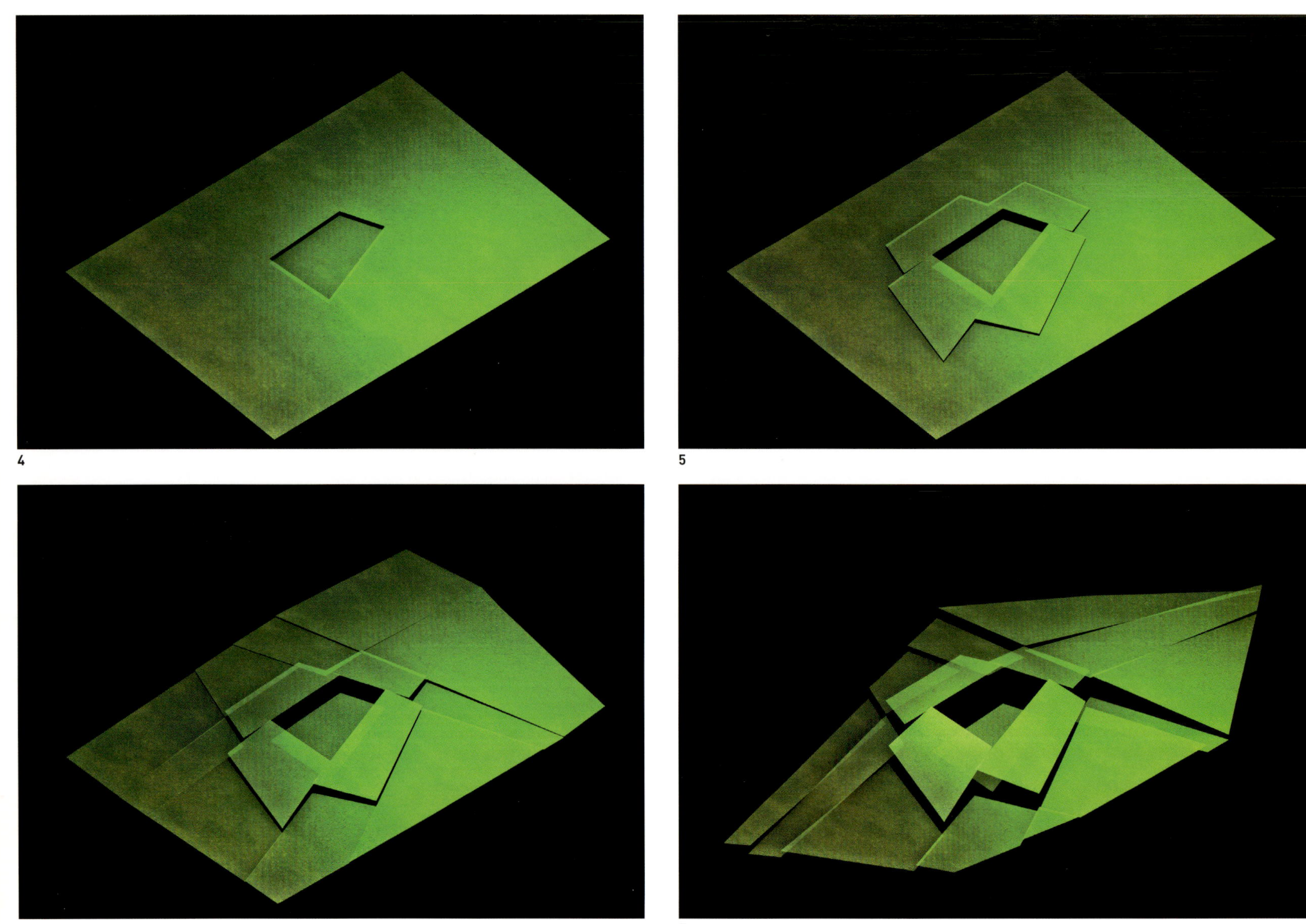

4
5
6
7

4–7 Generated surface geometries
8 Puzzle housing plan

This project was about designing a new theatre auditorium in an existing theatre and as a result, correcting two major problems of the old theatre, namely poor sight lines and bad acoustics.

JAKOB + MACFARLANE

The background to the building fabric we were required to work with lies in a series of nineteenth-century buildings that were combined, through demolition of their common walls, at the beginning of the twentieth century. The single space created housed a cinema, which in turn was converted to a National Theatre in the 1970s.

Our concept proposed the creation of a totally new skin inside the existing building, a kind of new 'stomach' morphed from successive layers of history. The design solution called for a sequence of 'cutting and slicing' interventions in order to develop this new interior space, and to meet the needs of changed site lines, along with increasing the rake angle of seating.

In approaching the refurbishment in this way, we created a series of folded timber planes that define the acoustic space of the auditorium; these timber planes also support the lighting and technical bridges overhead. In turn, the folded planes envelop the public by aligning and creating the stepped floor increments that provide platforms for the seating.

We employed the colour red as both a play on the history of the once-communist neighbourhood, and also as an appropriation or deformation of a typically bourgeois colour for theatre space. The result is a kind of strange red binocular object, a new theatre-machine created from juxtaposing histories.

1   Digital interior view of theatre
2 & 3   Digital morphed modelling

MAXIM GORKI THEATRE

1998

Normandy, France

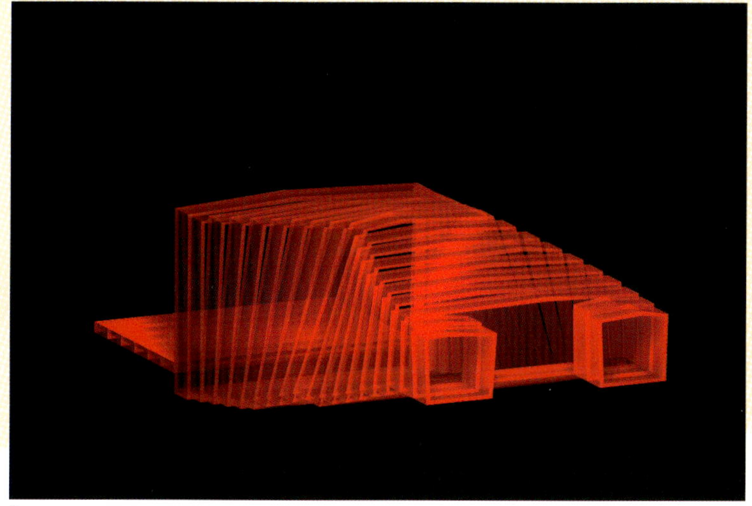

2

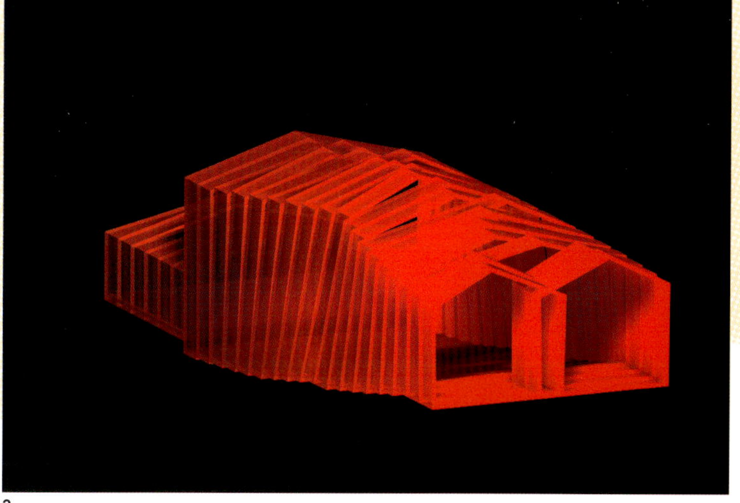

3

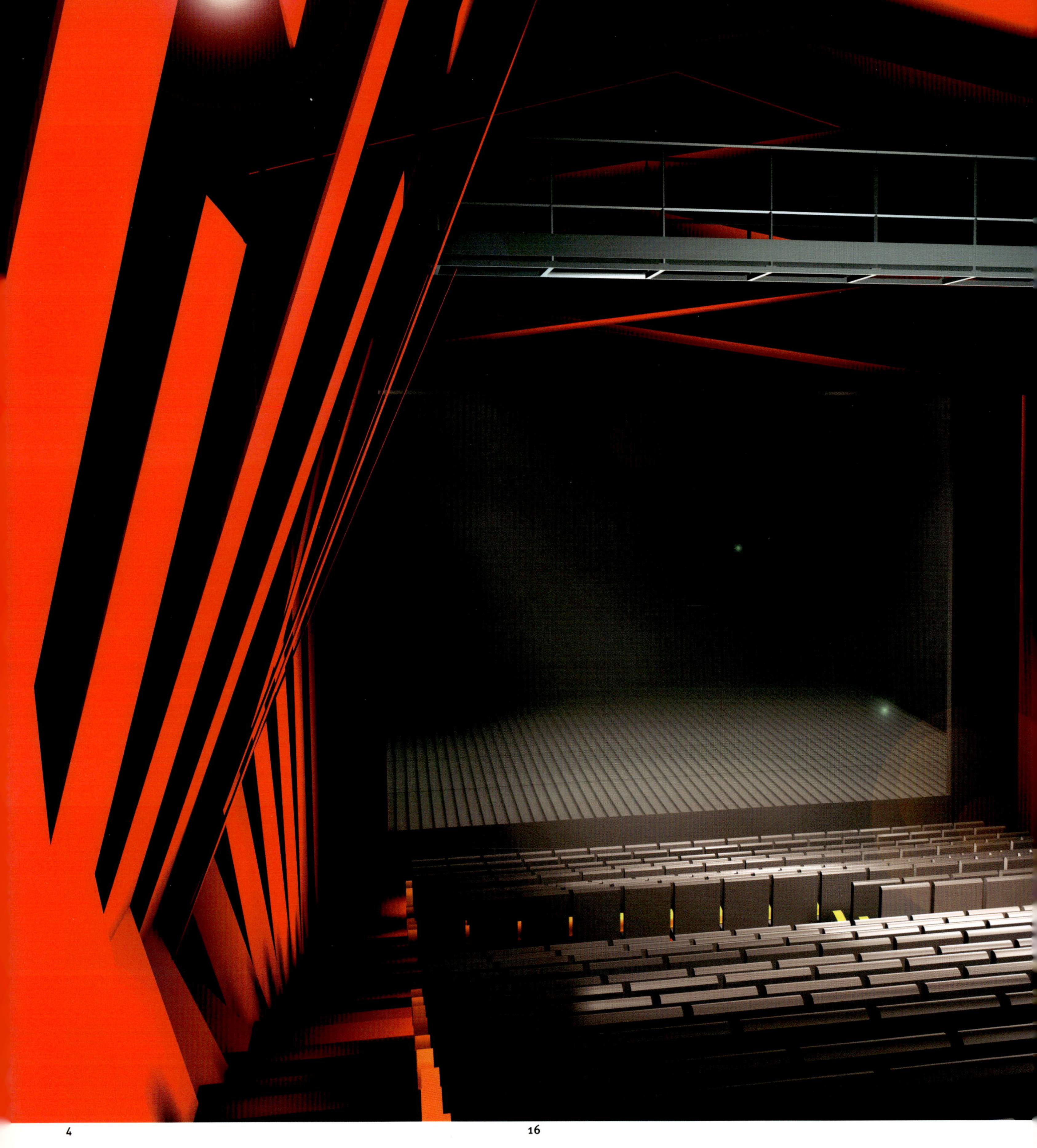

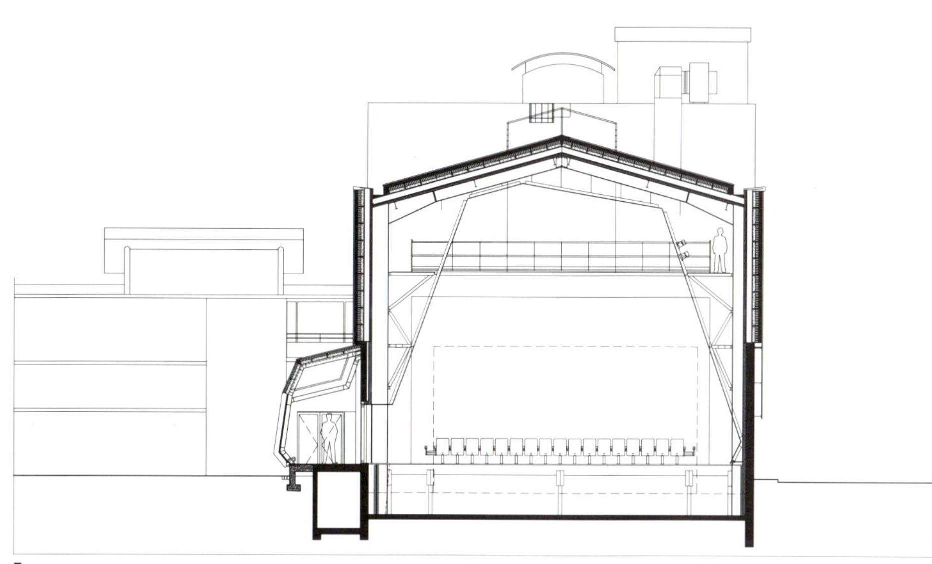

5

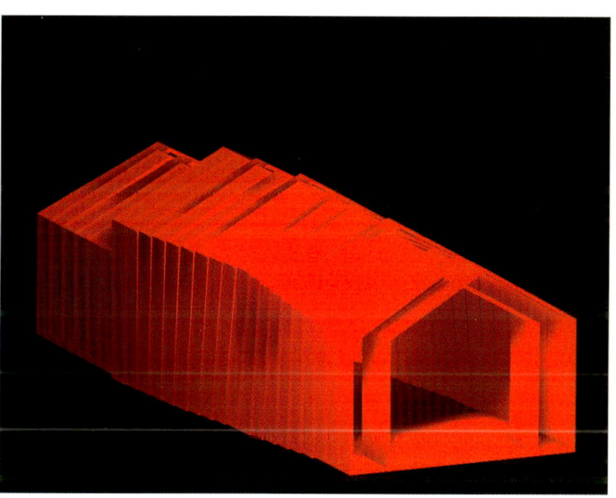

6

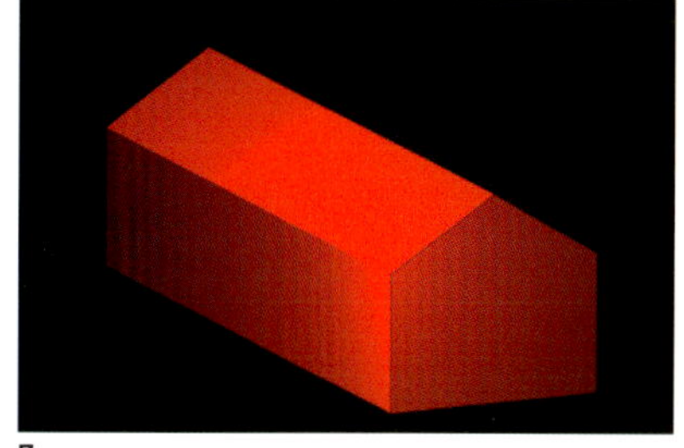

7

4   Digital interior view of theatre
5   Transversal section
6 & 7   Digital morphed modelling
Following pages:
Longitudinal section

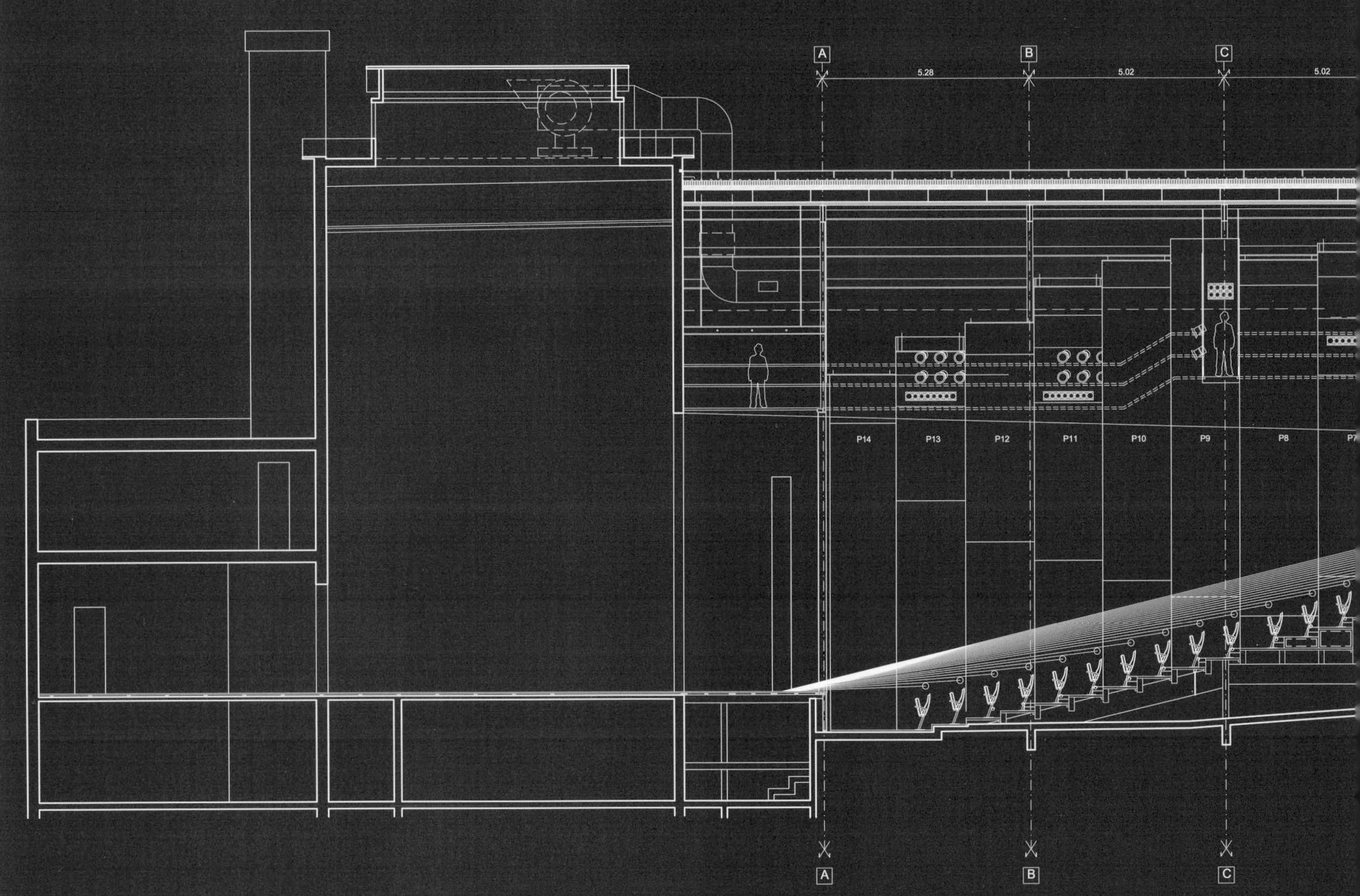

A
B
C
5.28
5.02
5.02
P14
P13
P12
P11
P10
P9
P8
P7
A
B
C

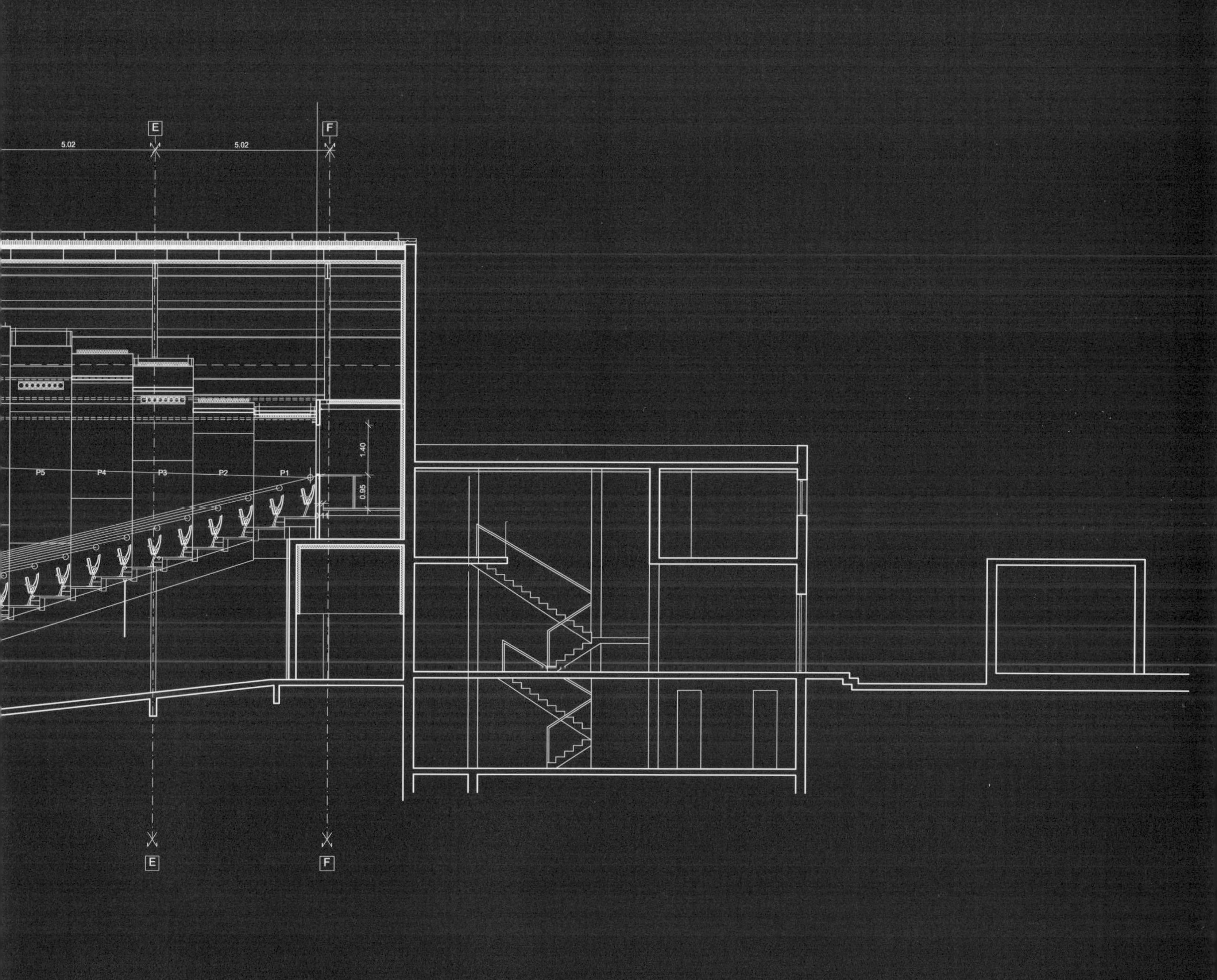

E
F
5.02
5.02
1.40
0.95
P5
P4
P3
P2
P1
E
F

9

10

9   Left hand entry – built project
10   Right hand entry – built project
11   Floor plan
12   Auditorium space – built project

EXISTANT
INTERVENTION PROJET
EXISTANT
A
A
PLACES
DEMONTABLES

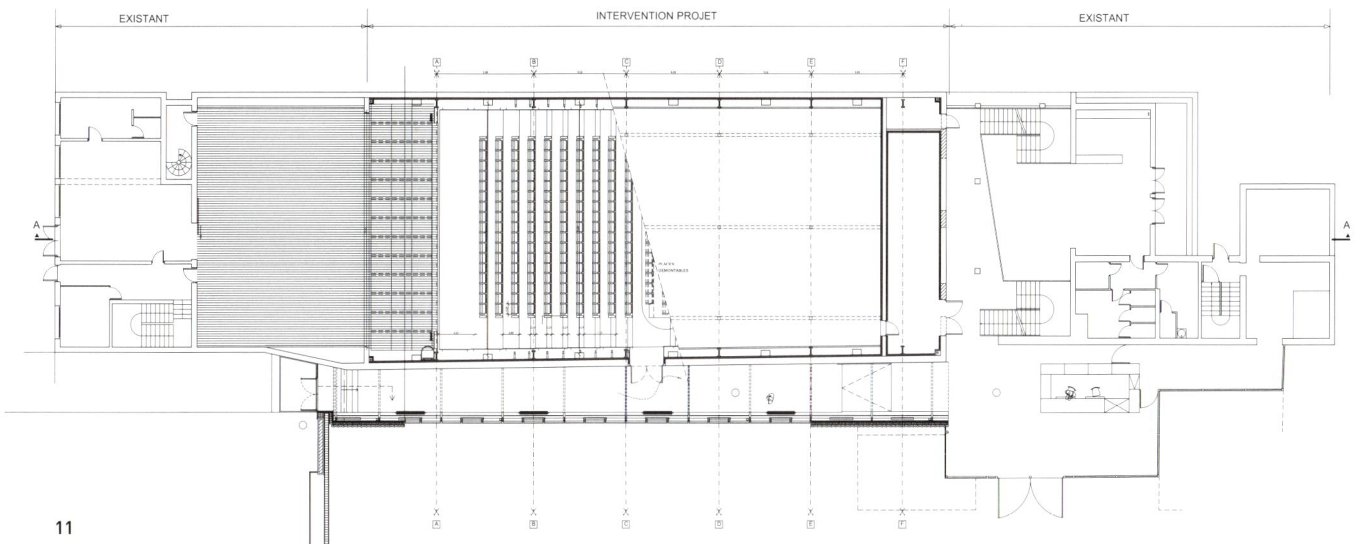

11

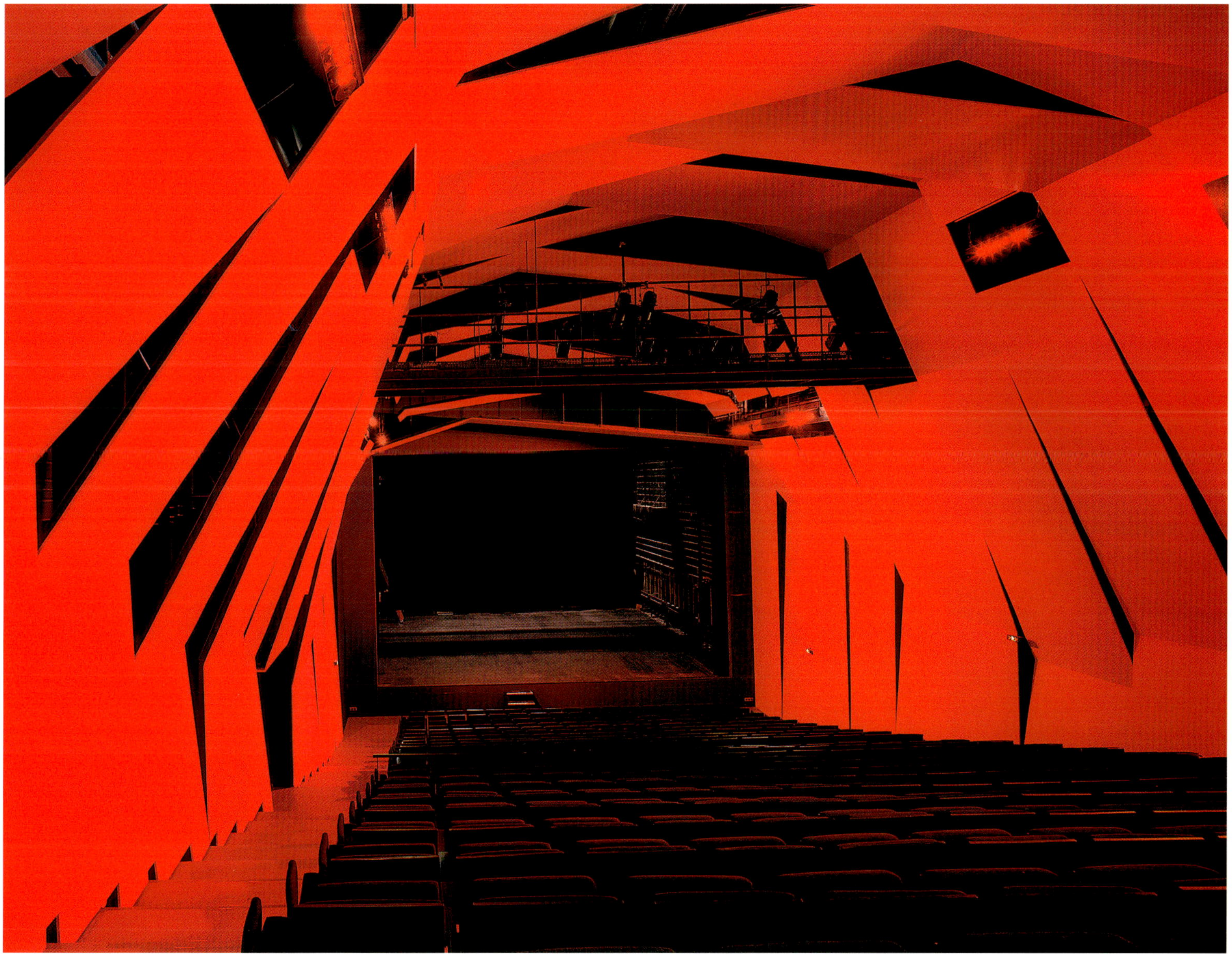

12

After an initial project in 1994 involving the remodelling of an existing house in the suburbs of Paris, this second extension/remodelling project on the same house, known as 'T House', incorporated the addition of an extra floor to this initial extension, creating a 40-square-metre loft space for the client's children.

It was decided to signify this second addition on the already built original extension of the house by giving it a different identity. We decided to offer the couple's young children two igloos made of zinc, perched on the roof of the existing house, as a way to represent their growing personal identity.

The completed project involves an enclosing envelope made of zinc, partially broken up into several volumes. Council regulations dictated our formal strategy by employing necessary setbacks and site-specific views from both inside and out. The result is a dovetailing of volumes that create a series of openings with complex geometric forms, offering views both skyward and towards the street.

1   View of roof-top addition from street

T HOUSE

1998

La Garenne Colombes, Paris, France

1

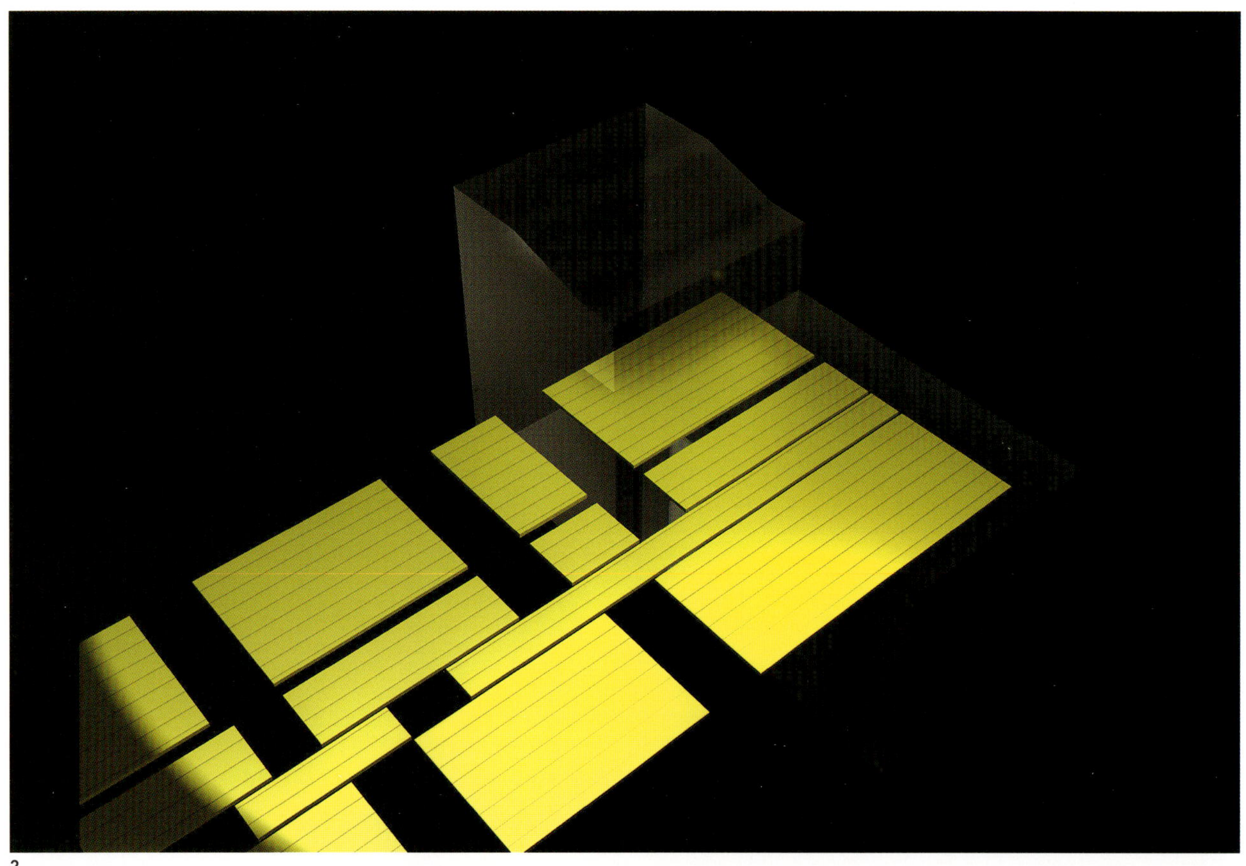

2

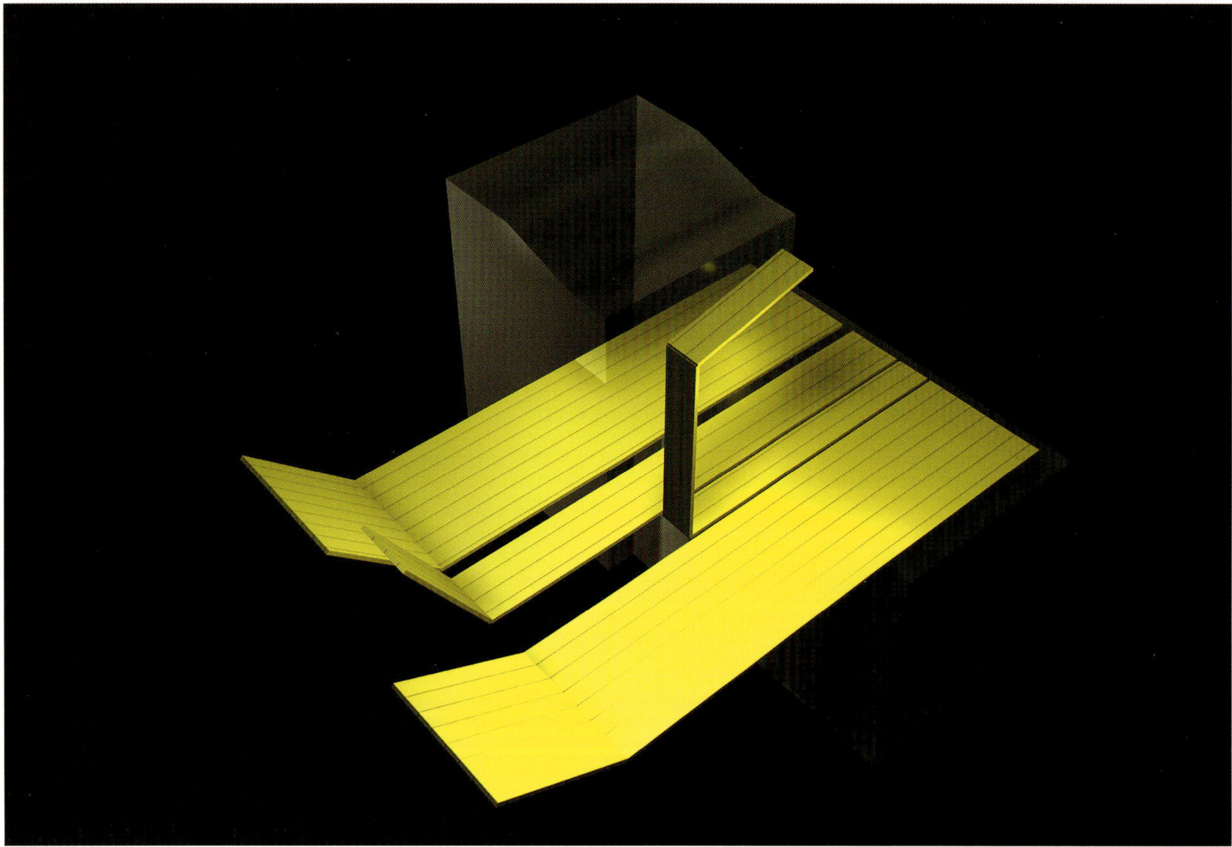

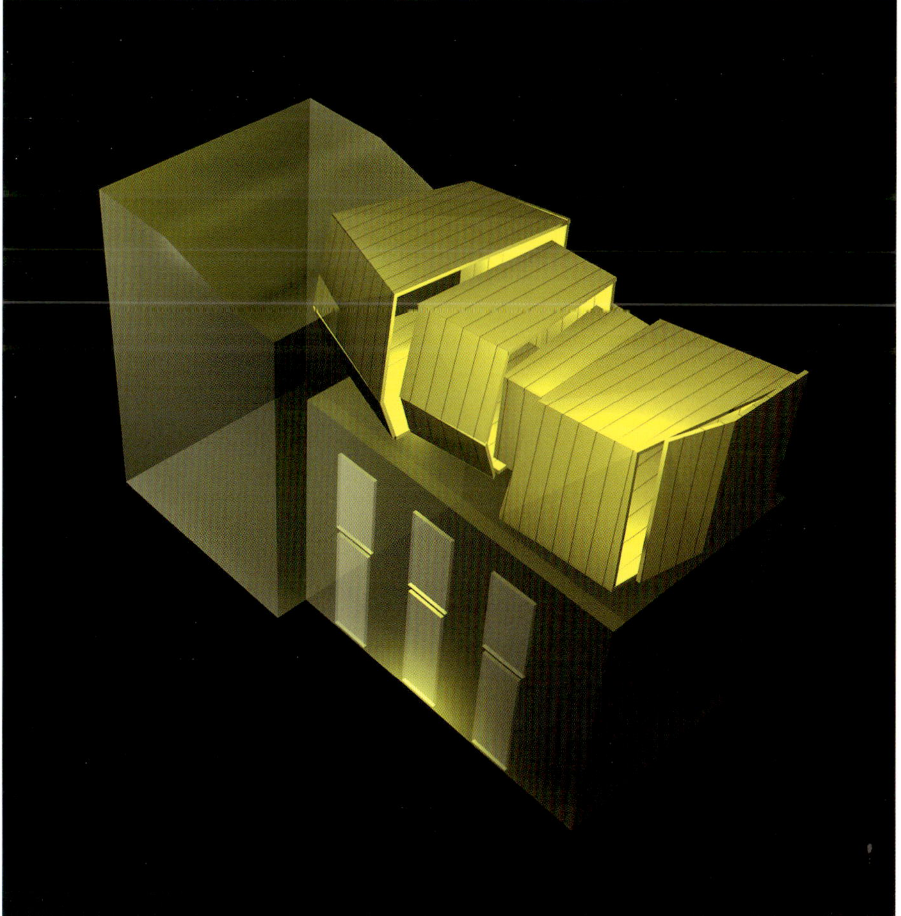

2–5 Conceptual sequence of generating volumes

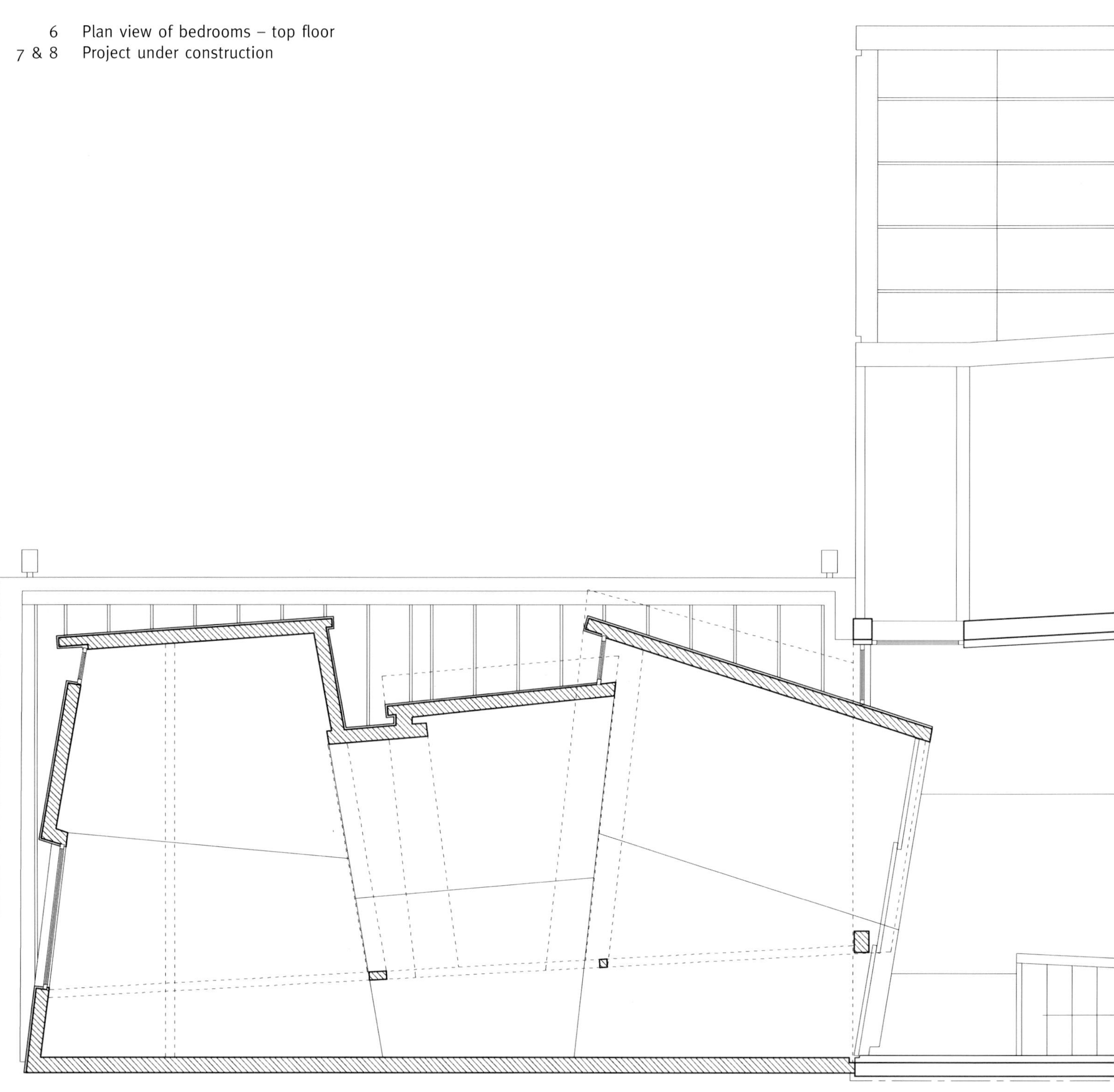

6

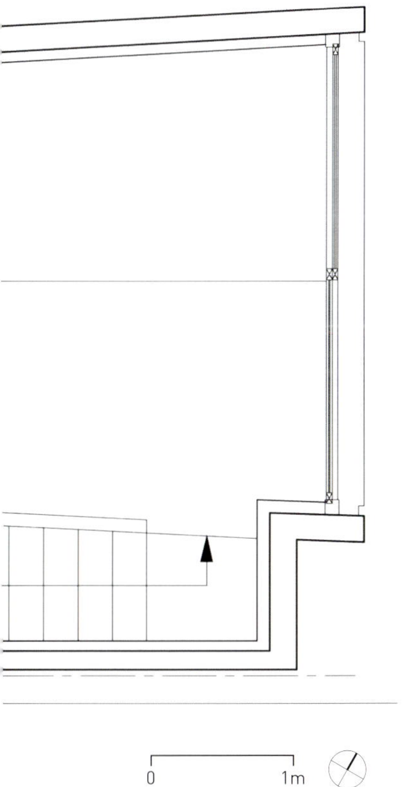

7

8

9

10

11

12

13

9–11   Project under construction
12 & 13   Exterior zinc cladding – construction phase
14   Interior light detail between two walls

14

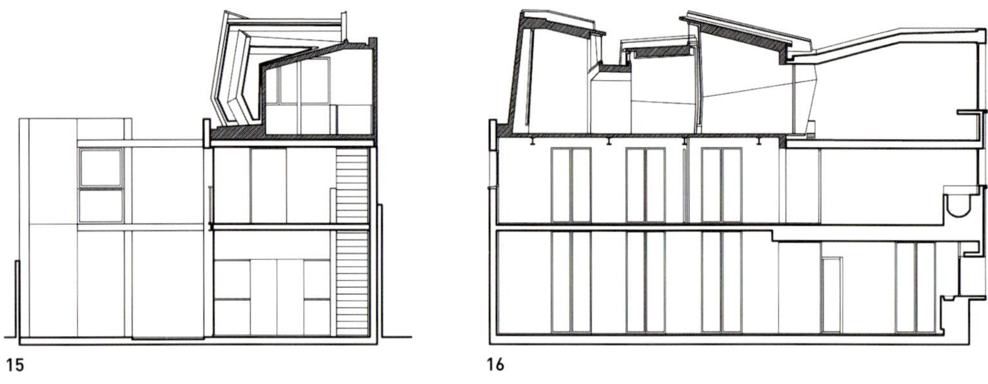

15

16

17

18

15 Transversal section
16 Longitudinal section
17–19 Interior views

19

The Branly Museum site is at an important bend in the Seine River in central Paris, not far from the Eiffel Tower. Because of this location, we wanted to create a strong sense of movement in the design, approximating the natural movement of the river.

In contrast to the circulated brief, we proposed to create a museum experience where the visitor is able to view the collection as a whole, as opposed to breaking up the material into distinct cultural divisions. We chose to resist a fixed historical reading of the exhibits in our design proposal, proposing instead a museum space where the collections could be read and reread as ongoing historical research.

As a result, we chose the metaphor of a forest to guide our design thinking. This forest metaphor suggested a new way to create paths in and around the collections on display. As opposed to the type of path where one encounters artifacts grouped in their historical periods, creating 'clumps' of forest, we were more interested in creating a path that resulted in a more random and personal encounter with the exhibits, a kind of criss-crossing of time and experience. The circulation system we envisioned created a more informal experience dotted with revelation and surprises – an experience of discovery and of newfound knowledge.

The proposed building volume would be an immense field of solid and void space, which fills the site using radial elements as the generating geometrical base for all building systems. The exterior cladding of the building would be constructed in stainless steel to create a dialogue with the urban condition of its context. The interior walls, floor and ceiling would be surfaced in a renewable timber, similar in materiality to the artifacts and collections being exhibited.

BRANLY MUSEUM

Competition entry, 1999

Paris, France

1

2

3

1 Final plan
2 Site plan
3 Interior view
4 Model

4

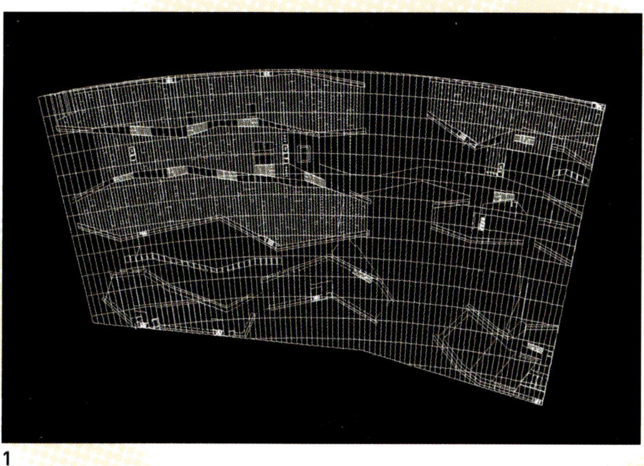

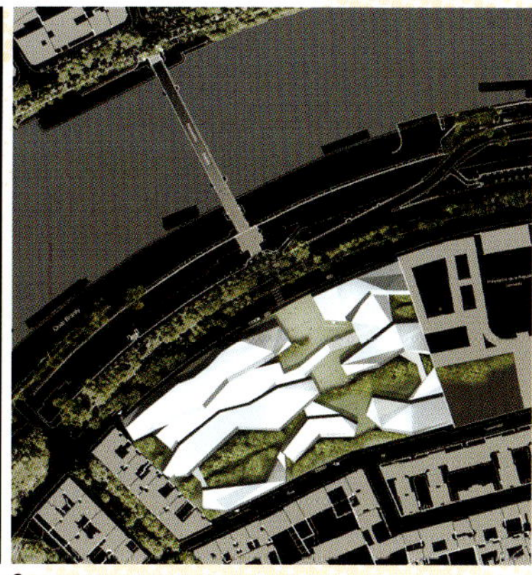

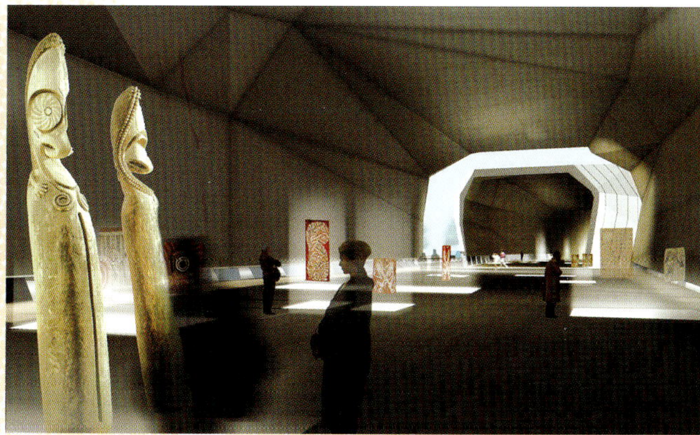

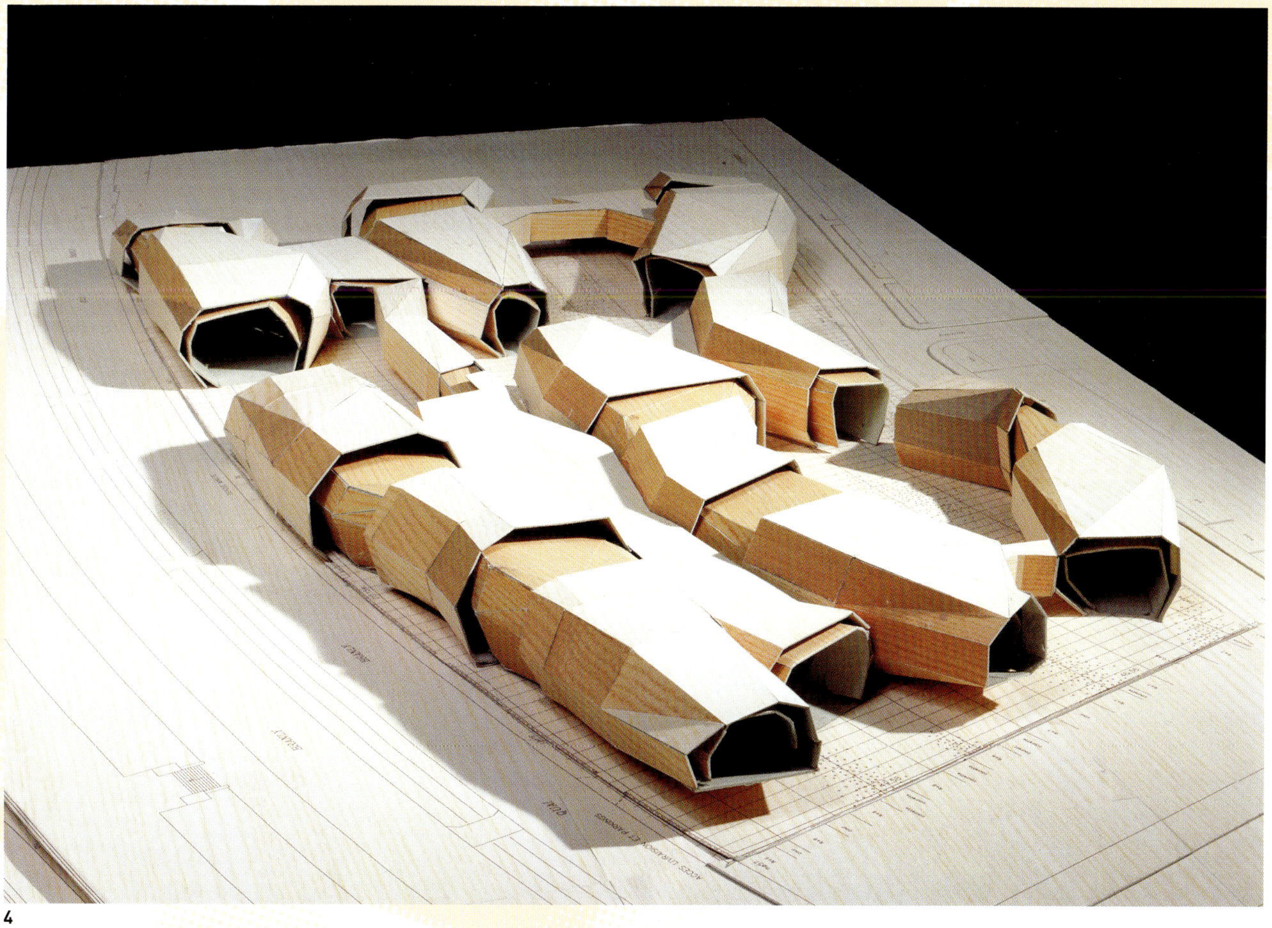

5

8

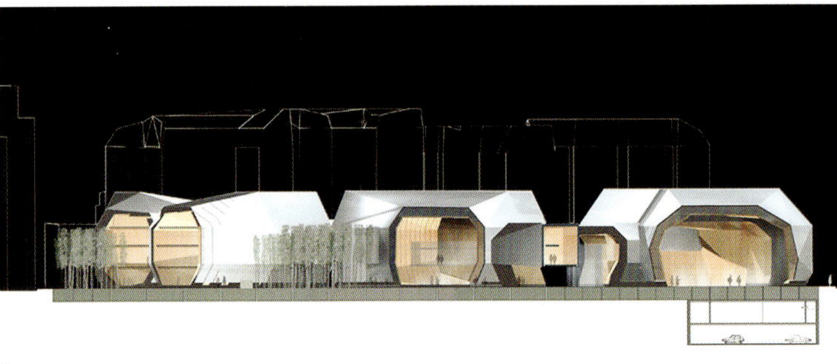

6

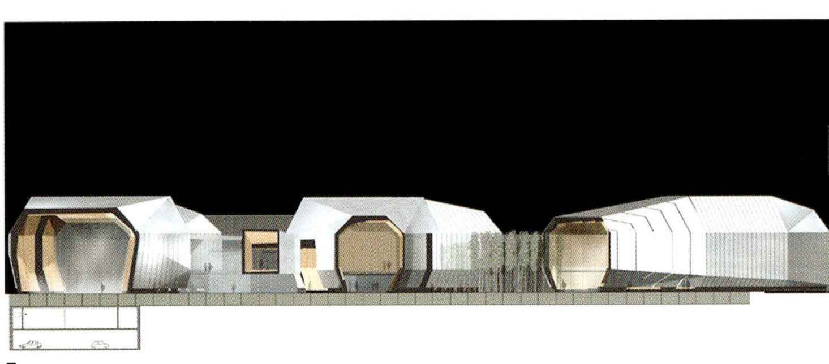

7

5   Street elevation
6   Entry elevation – west
7   Entry elevation – east
8   Interior view towards garden
9   Main façade view from Quai Branly

9

10

11

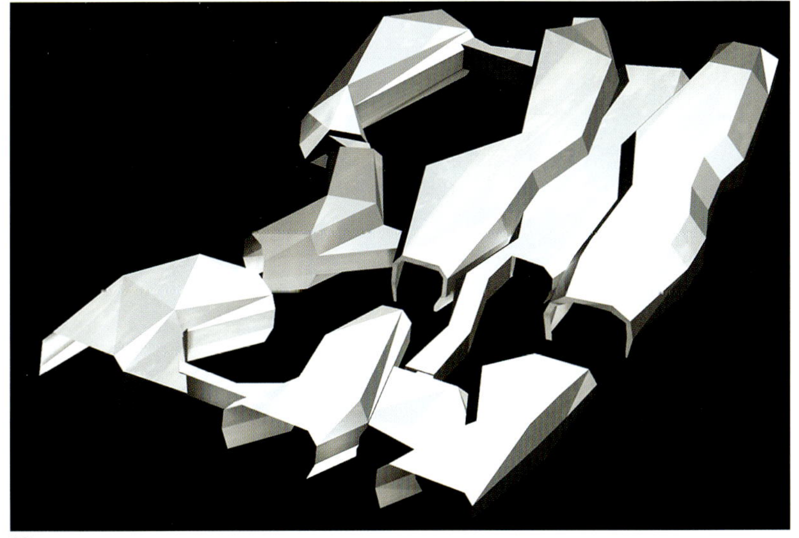

12

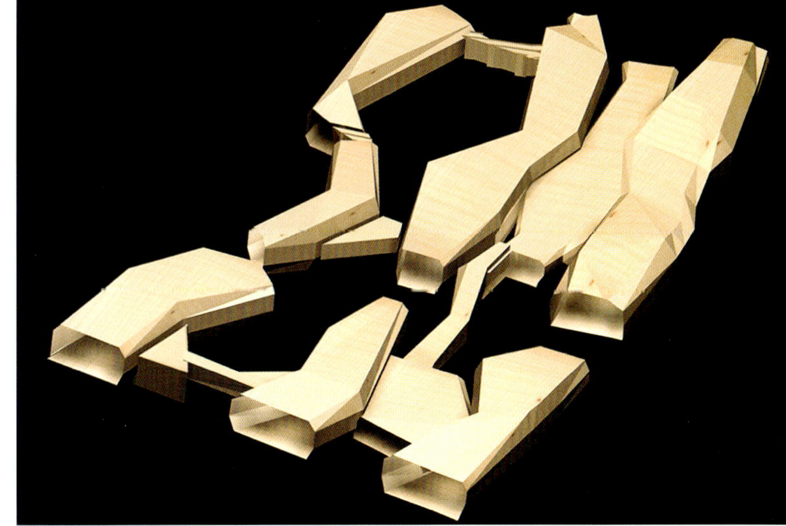

13

10 & 11   Photos of model
12   Exterior metal cladding – axonometric view
13   Interior wooden floor wall ceiling surfaces – axonometric view
14   Programmatic axonometric diagram

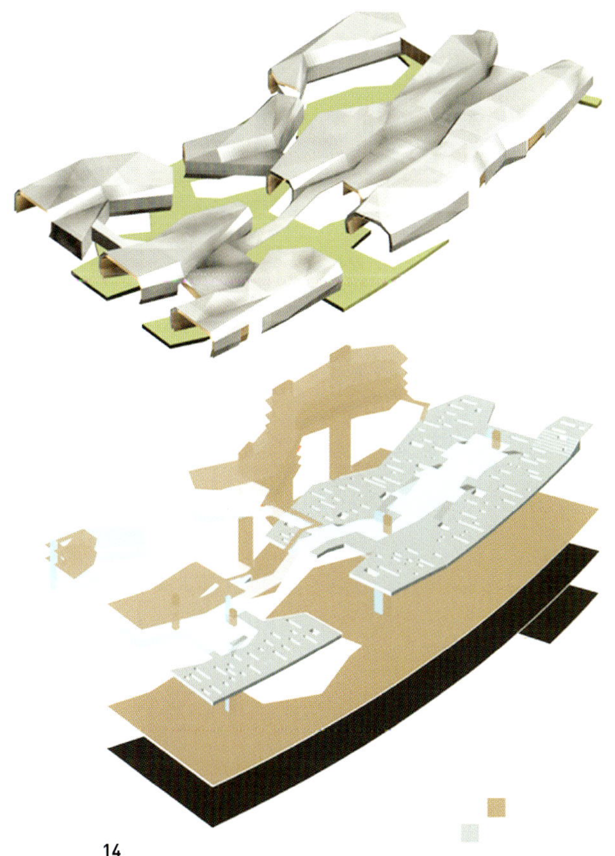

14

Our project is conceived as a new theatre auditorium created within the shell of an existing theatre building; or simply put, as an orange box inside an existing box. In our design approach to the project, all the primary concrete structural elements of Novarina's original building were retained intact. We intervened in such a way as to express and accentuate this existing simple concrete structure. The intention was to read the new project as an intervention.

The orange box is in reality a long folding and wrapping wall that announces the new interior space of the auditorium. It is designed to give the auditorium space the correct acoustic, climatic and spatial qualities.

The new auditorium plan creates three types of stage configuration in order to bring the difficult configuration of the existing corner triangular stage out into, and surrounded by, the audience. The first configuration uses a temporary proscenium stage that creates an overall deep stage; the second configuration utilises the existing triangular stage with increased seating in the proscenium space; the third configuration utilises closed-off walls behind the proscenium in order to create the most intimate stage condition of the three variations.

Metal cladding chosen for this wall evokes the industrial clad agricultural buildings that are readily found in this region. It is used in this project to define a cultural space. This design approach was chosen in order to break down the formality of the theatre, and turn it into a space that might be more readily engaged by the community.

The orange colour of the metal cladding references a typical French construction site, thus helping to create another reading of the theatre as a place of action, fabrication and drama. In the evening, the colour becomes a sign for the community, signalling the beginning of a performance.

THE ORANGE BOX THEATRE

1998

Pont-Audemer, Normandy, France

2

3

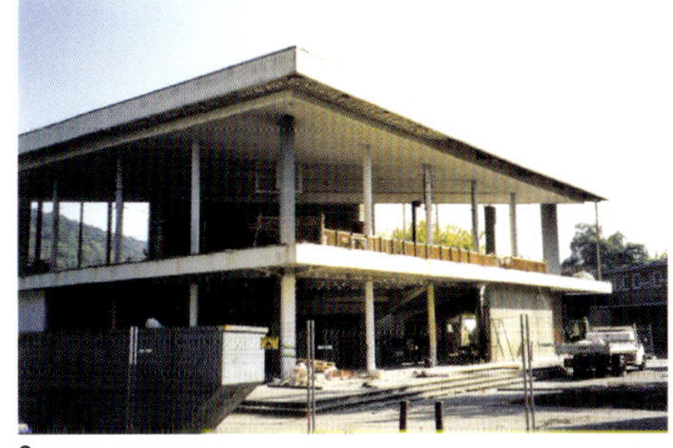

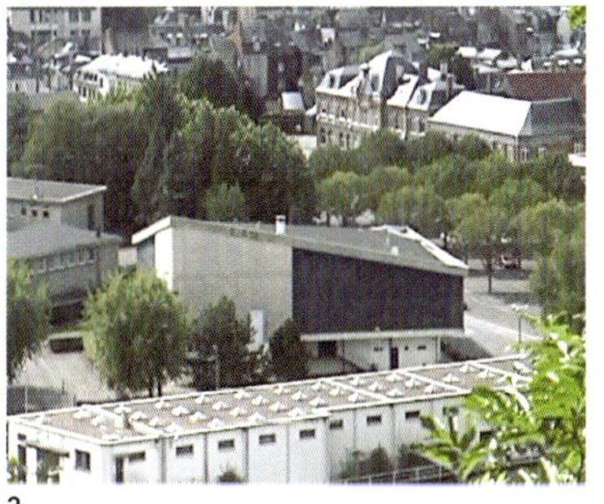

1 Finished exterior
2 & 3 Theatre before intervention

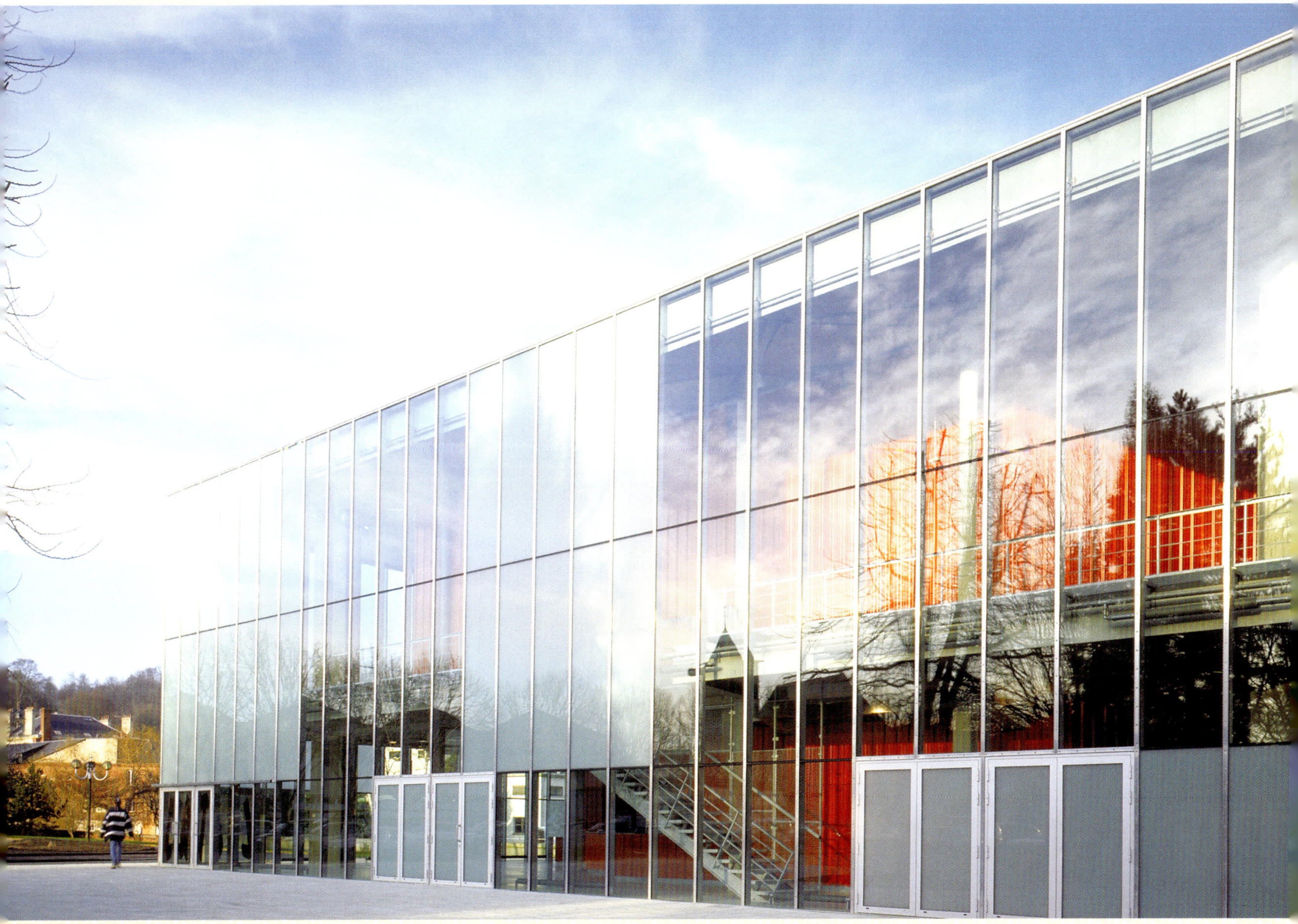

1

4

4 Exterior elevation at night
5 Site plan and first floor plan showing auditorium and stage

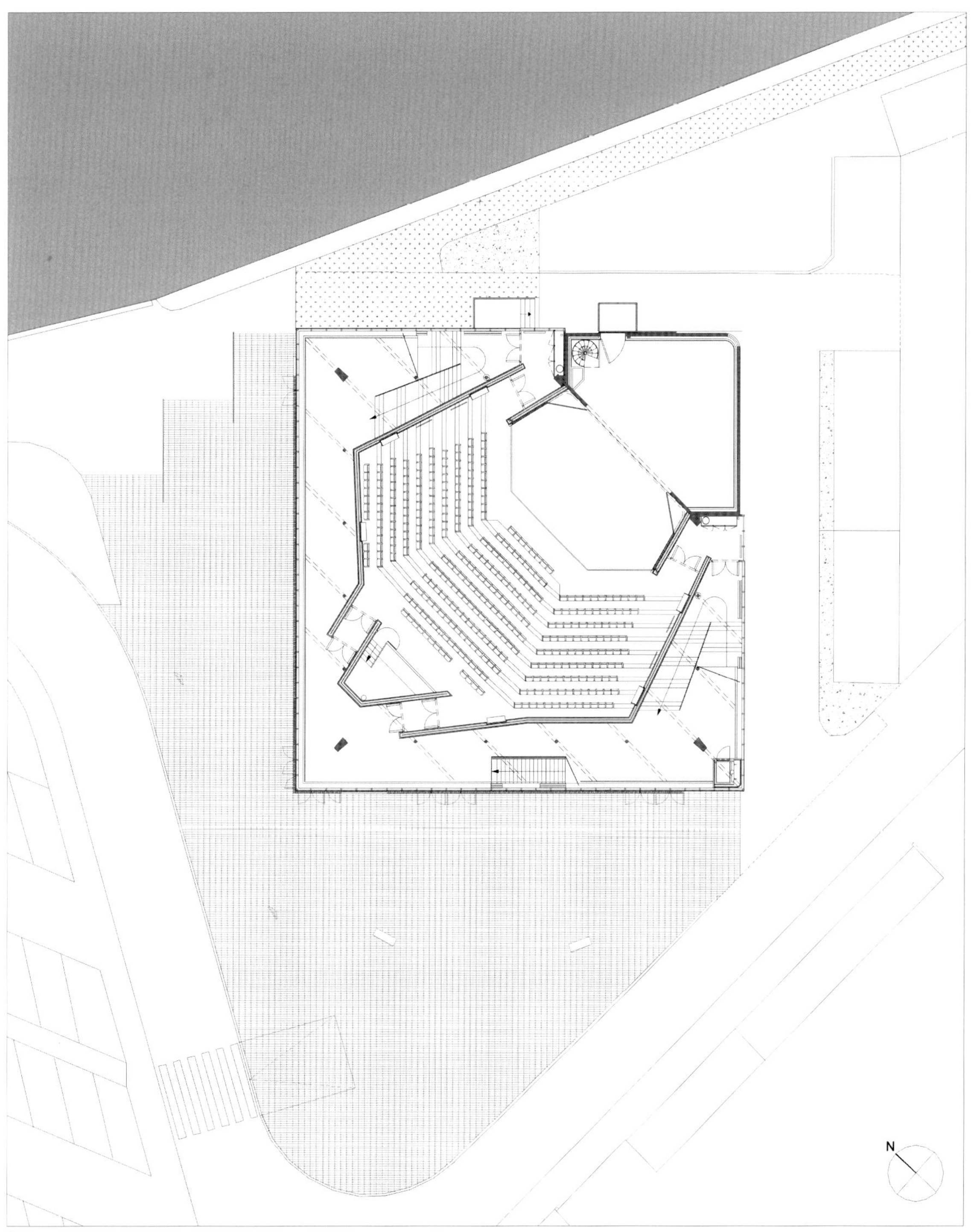

N

6 & 8   Exterior at night
7   Longitudinal section

6

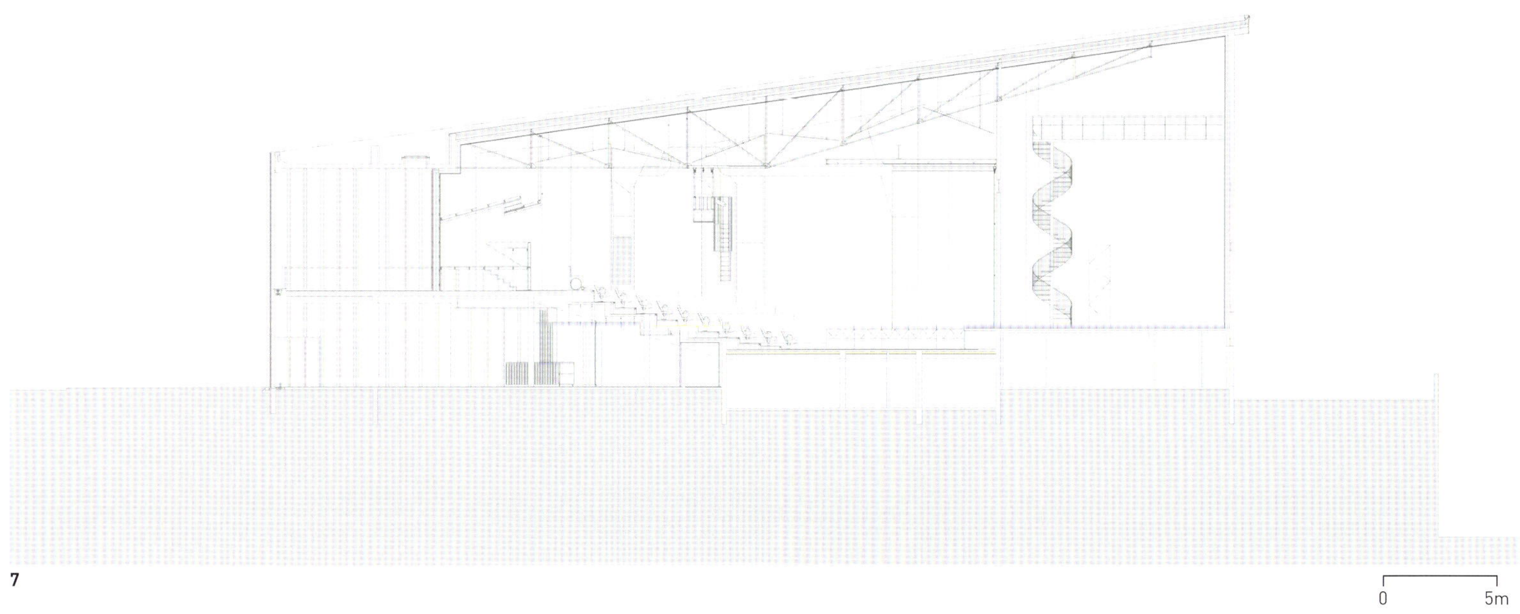

7

8

9

10

11

13   First floor with existing concrete columns
14   Entrance ticket office and counter
15   View of side stairs from first floor
16   Ground floor space with existing columns

13

14

15

16

17   Exterior from adjacent river
18   View of auditorium and projectionist booth
19   View of auditorium and stage

18

19

The brief for this project was to create a restaurant on the sixth floor of the Georges Pompidou Centre, a project that would need to contain all the usual programmatic requirements associated with a restaurant, opening out onto an exterior roof terrace.

In conceptualising the project, we became interested in the notion of trying to create architecture that responded in some way to what was already given on the site. Not wanting to import or create an obvious addition to the site's architectural context, we proposed the lightest possible intervention. Our interest was to discover or insert a kind of non-existent or background presence, an almost non-architectural or non-designed response. It was through this desire that we became interested in working with the floor surface, proposing this surface as a new field of intervention, deforming it so that we could insert a series of volumes beneath it, thus creating a new landscape of both interior and exterior conditions. We proposed to construct the floor surface or 'skin' for the project from aluminium, a material, which when brushed, both absorbs and reflects light, thus also reinforcing the notion of background presence, appearance and disappearance. This solution created minimal intervention, but with a strong personality – much like a mask.

The series of volumes created in the design process are slid beneath the skin of the floor: kitchen, bar, cloak room and private reception room, all finding their eventual form and position through the tried and tested negotiation process of design. The skin concept also led us to conceive a stretchable surface, which we could employ to 'absorb' all the variabilities of programme in the space. The design was then finalised, caught or frozen in a state of movement, achieved through the utilisation of digital design methods. The sense of movement in the space was something we wanted to capture, creating an architecture that records the dynamics of programme and actuality.

Another aspect of our response to the site, specifically the concept of using the floor as developable form, was in appropriating the existing building grid of the Pompidou Centre. The structure and surface increment of the floor is divisible into an 800 millimetre x 800 millimetre grid at the smallest level, up to the primary structure of 12.8 metres. We appropriated the combination of these constructional and structural grids as our 'conceptual' grid, which was then deformed by the volumes (or what we termed as pockets) inserted into the space.

A further approach to the design of the site was to work with the principle that all services enter the space via the ceiling and then drop into each created 'pocket', with each of the four pockets having their own internal 'life support systems' of air circulation, water access, electricity supply and information systems. This approach then became part of a broader intention to divert the building's infrastructure support services system and utilise it in the design of the space in a playful manner.

The furniture is designed in such a way that the top surface of all tables are aligned at 700 millimetres above the floor, in order to create a 'sea of furniture', realising a seamless extension between the inside and the outside roof terrace space.

RESTAURANT GEORGES, POMPIDOU CENTRE

2000

Paris, France

1

2

3

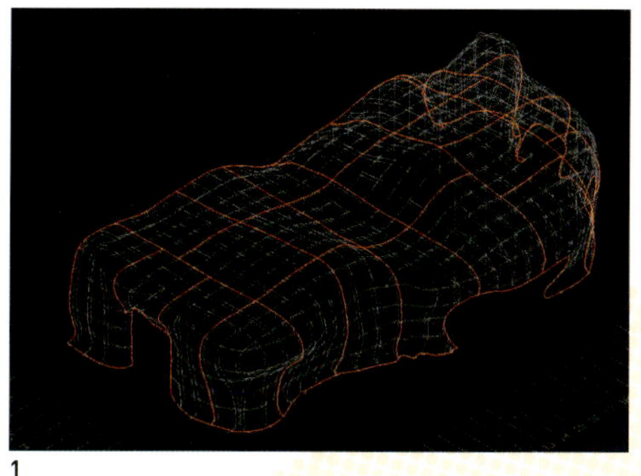

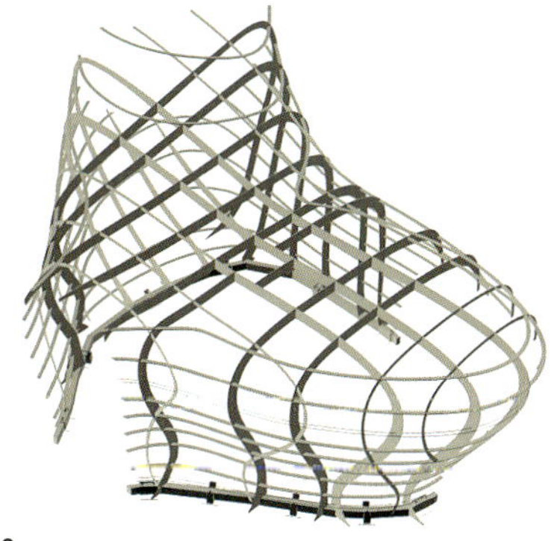

1 Digital modelling of structure – kitchen volume
2 Digital modelling of structure – bar volume
3 Interior view at night

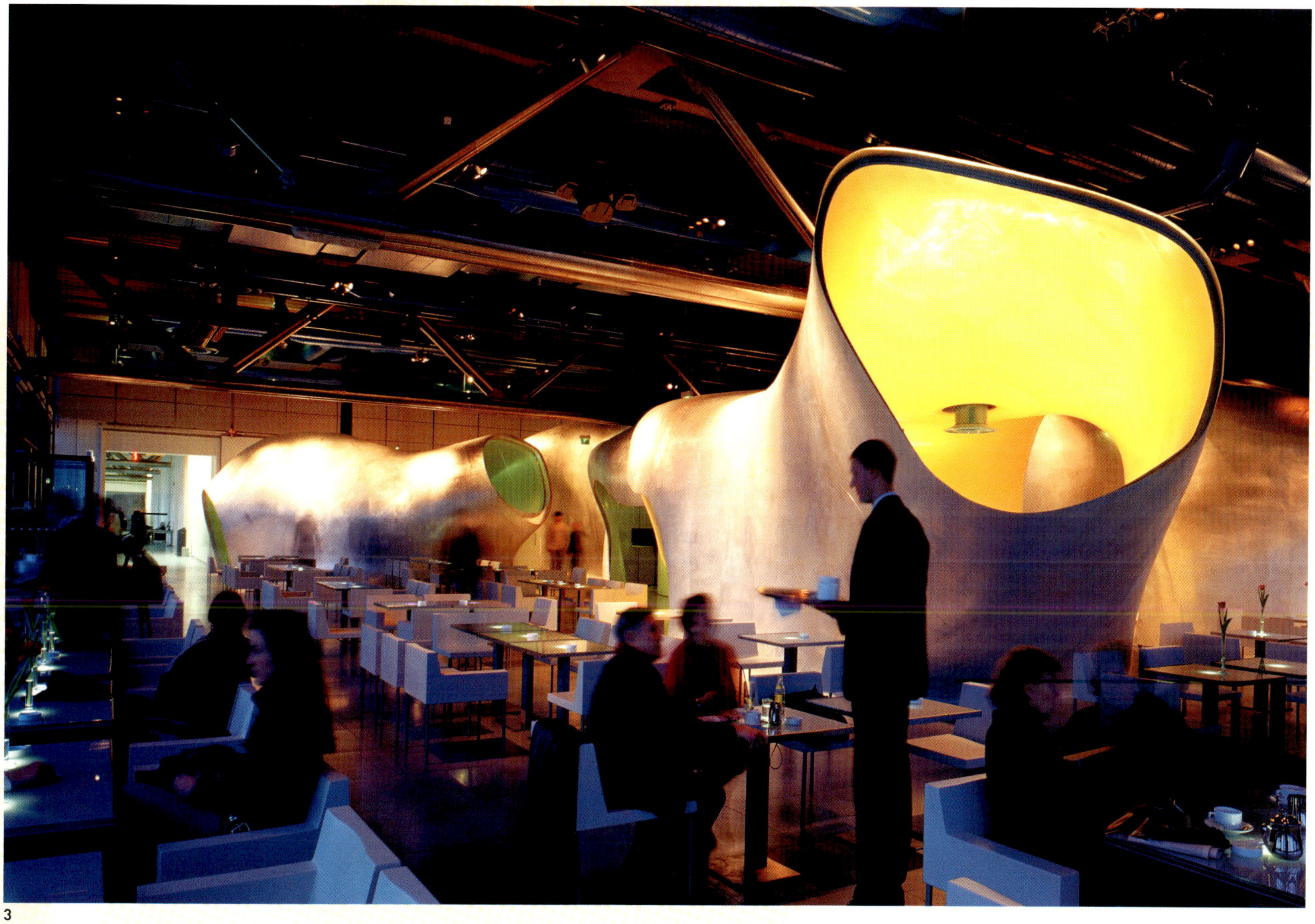

4

5

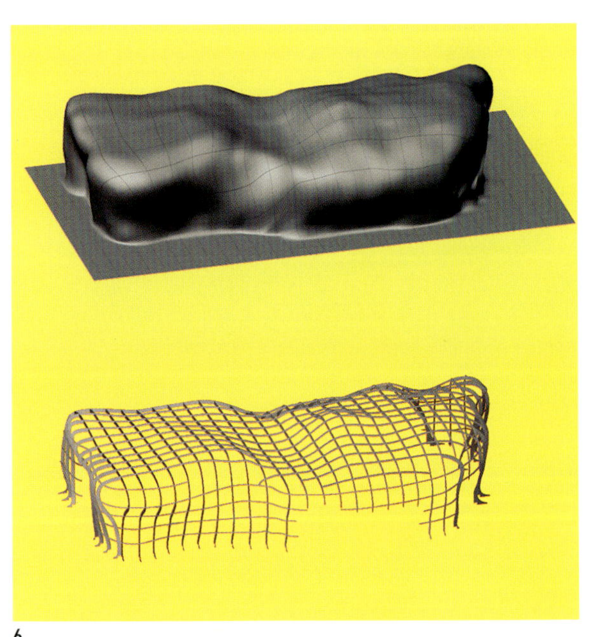

6

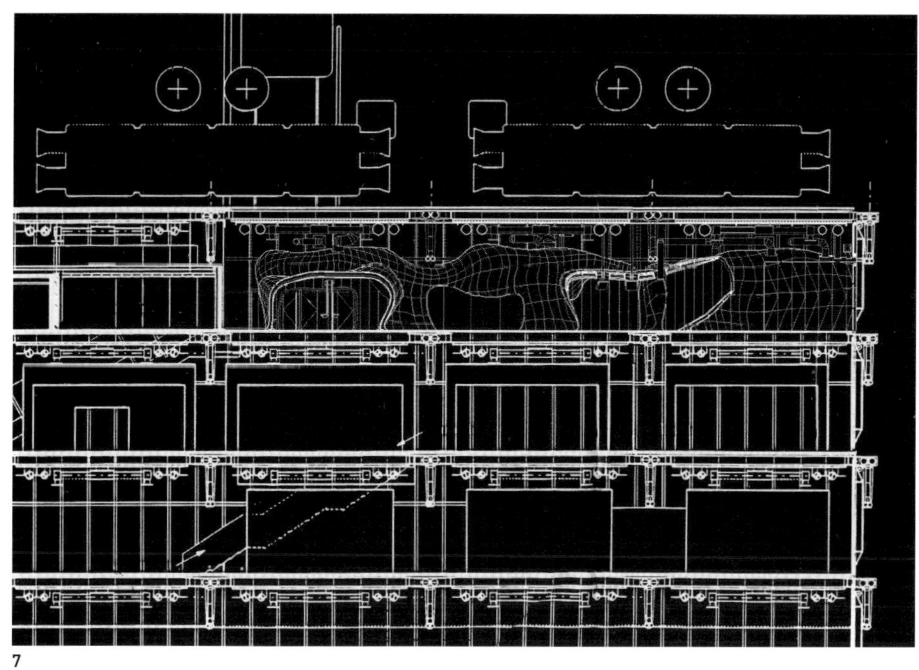

4   Conceptual sketches
5 & 6   Digital modelling of skin and structure
7   Longitudinal section through restaurant
        and museum
8   Conceptual sketches
9   Digital conceptual model
10   Plan of digital conceptual model

7

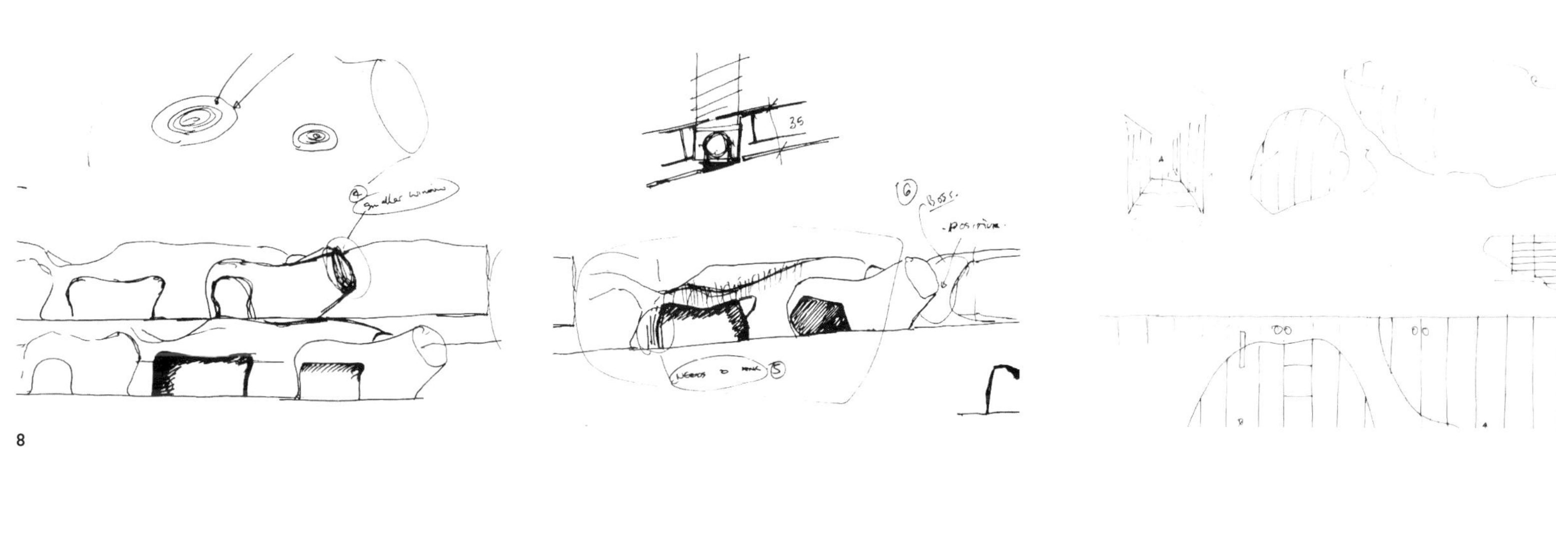

8

9

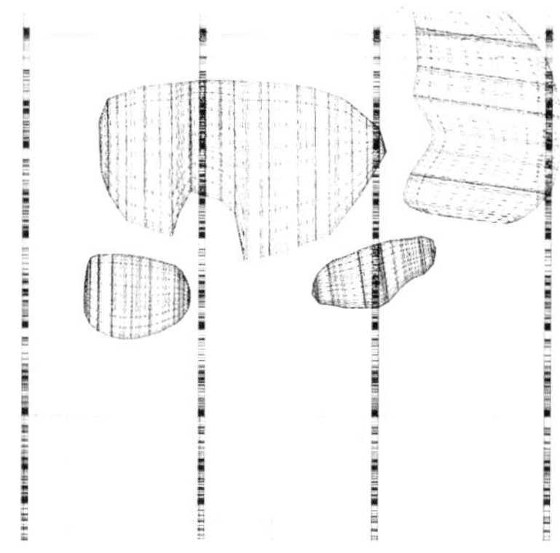

10

11

12

13

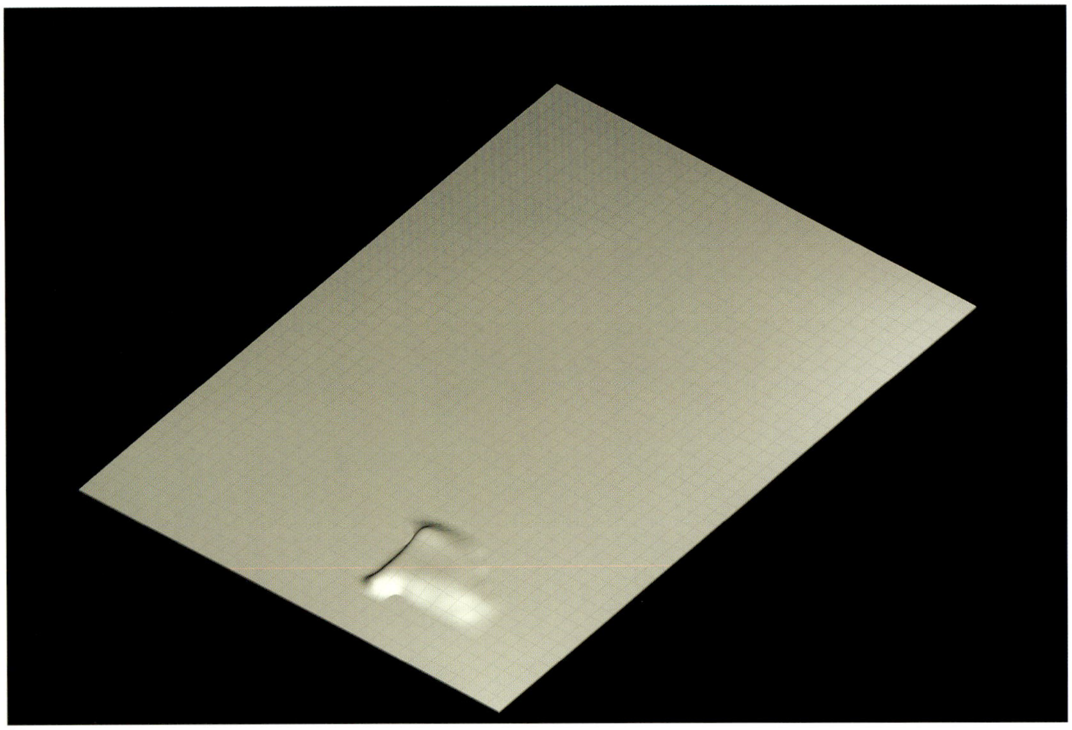

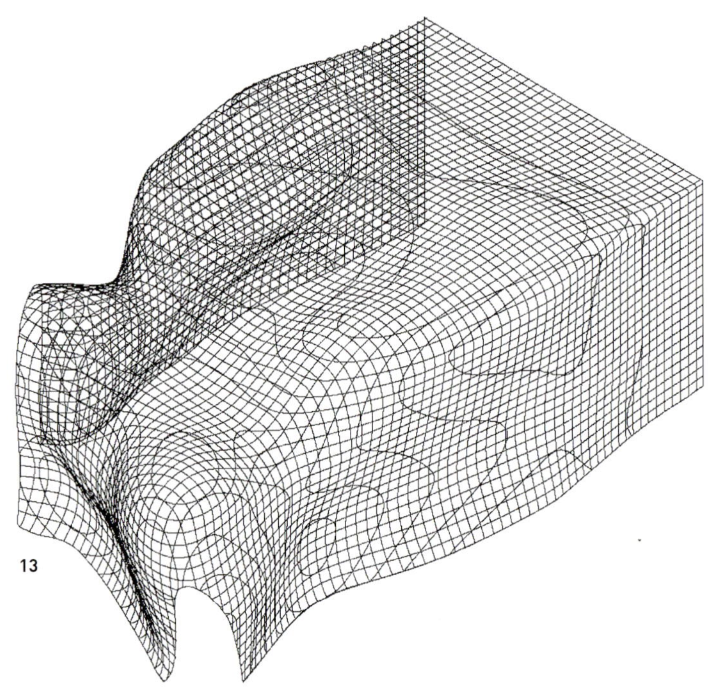

11,12,14,15 Conceptual film stills showing floor deformation
13 Structural engineering surface mesh study

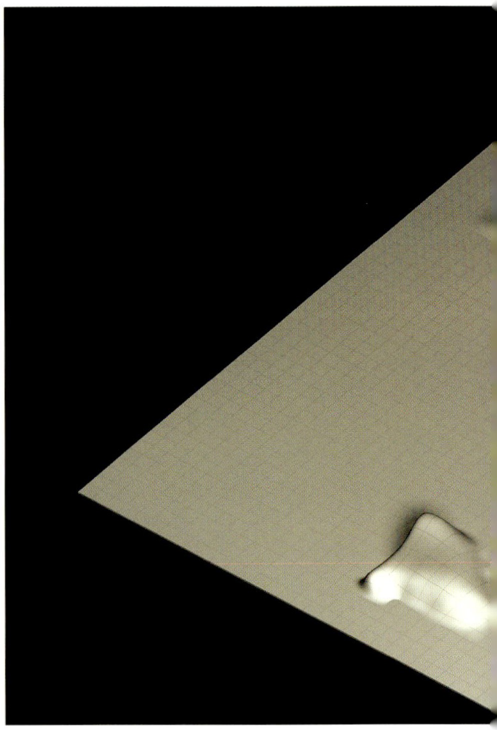

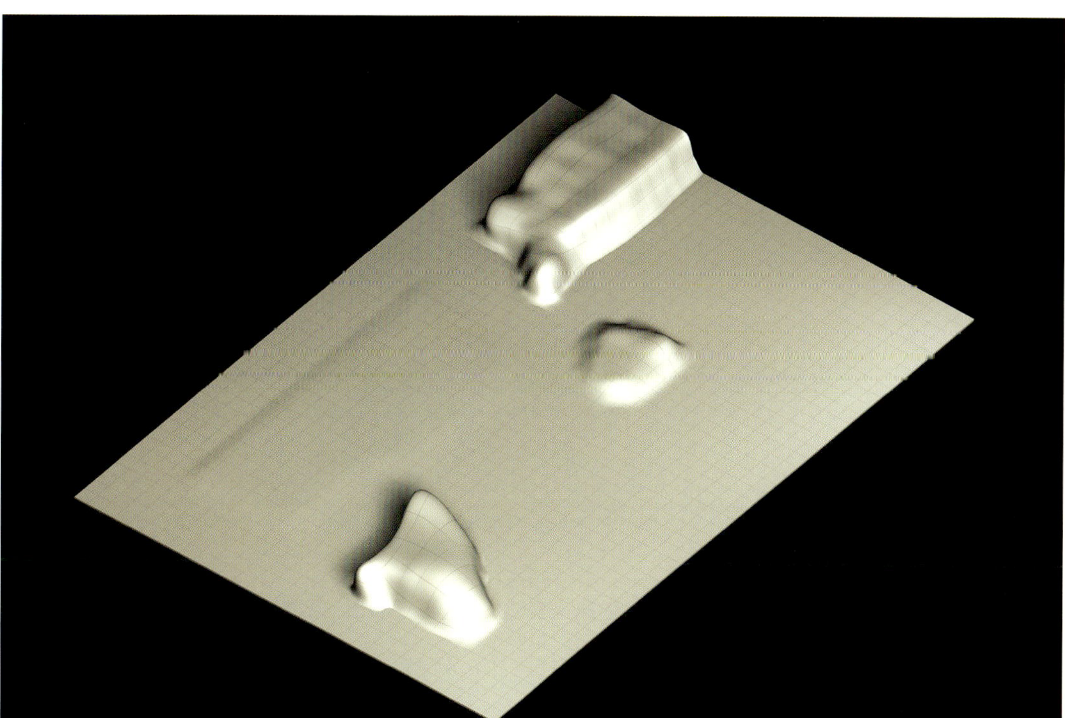

14

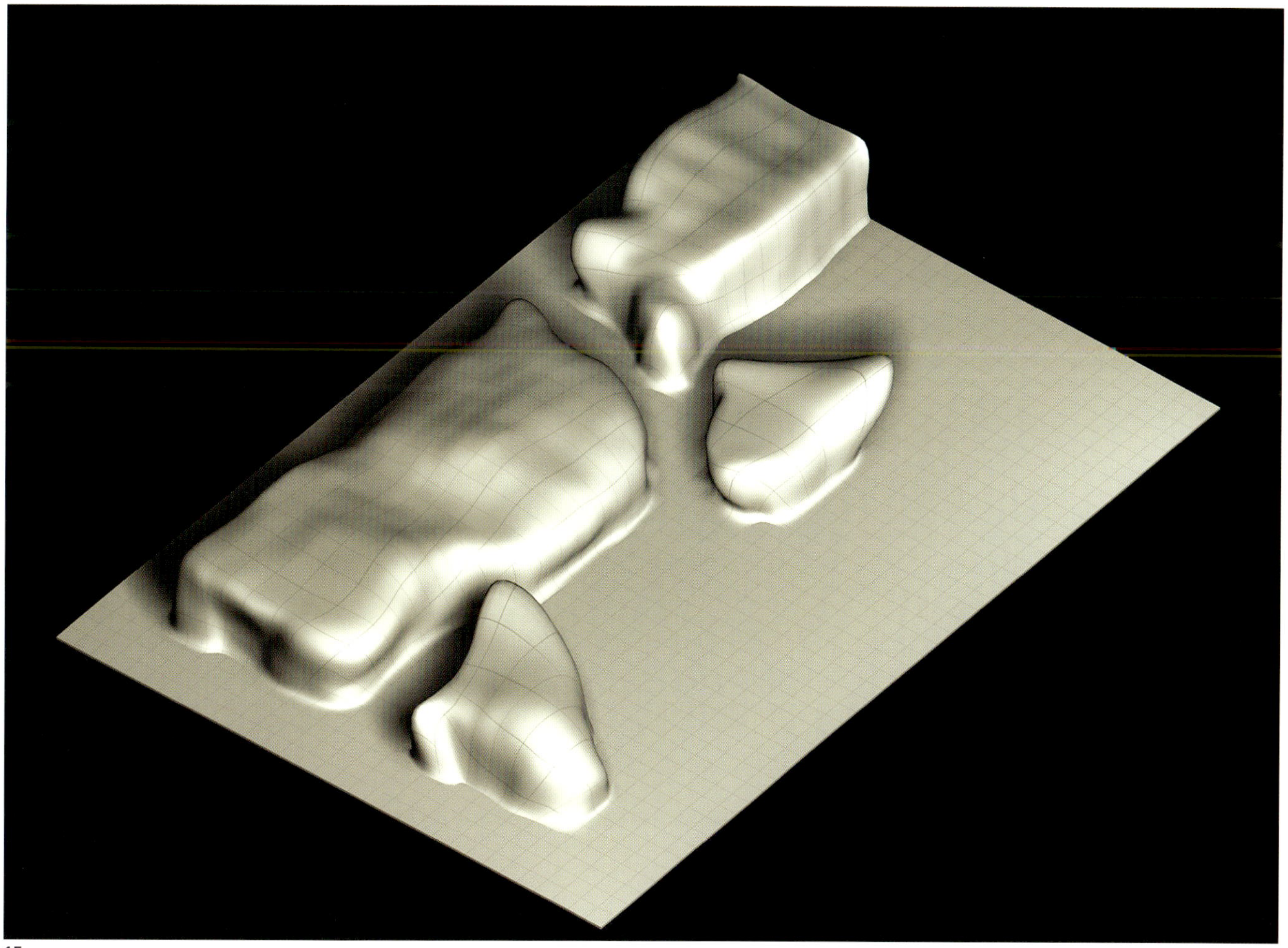

15

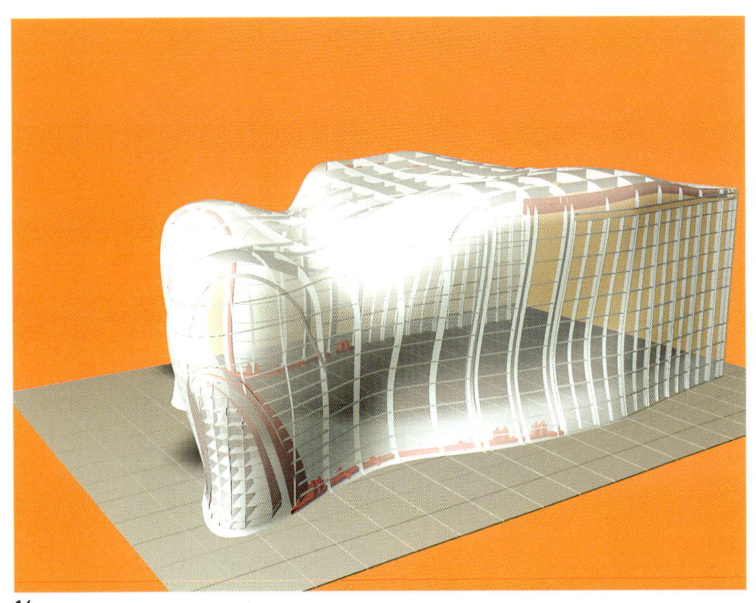

16

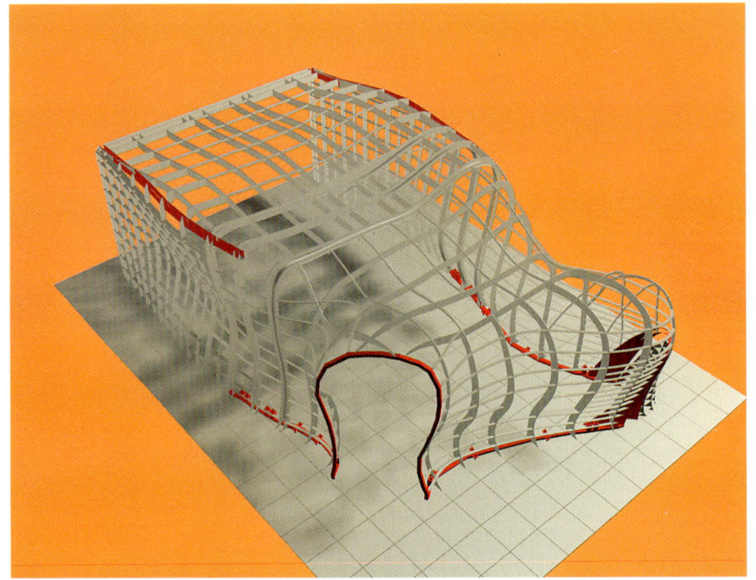

17

18

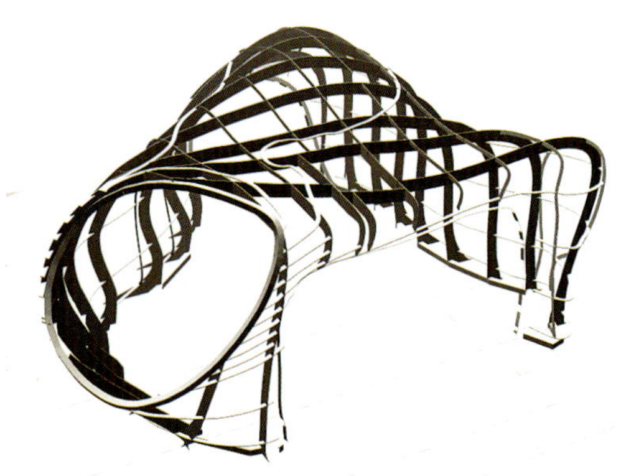

19

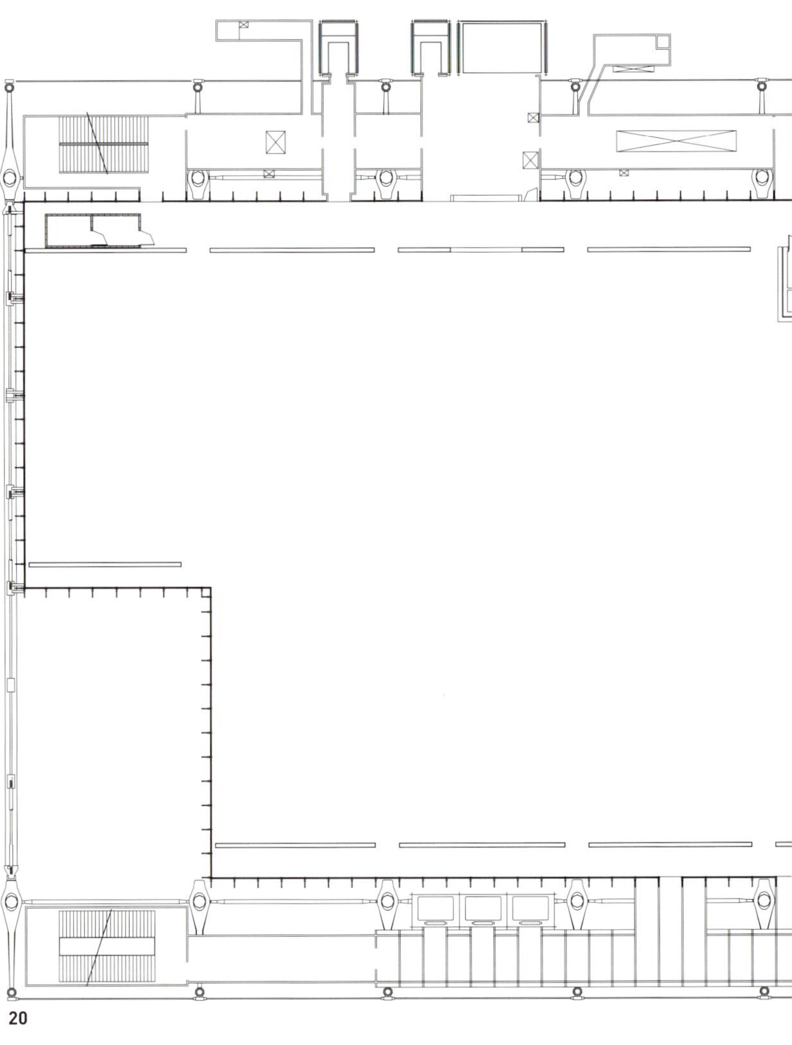

20

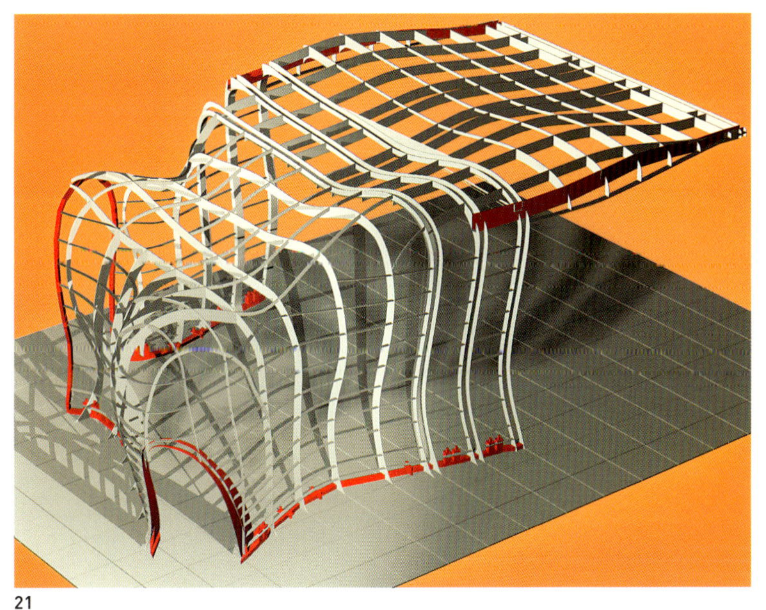

21

16,17,21   Red volume, skin and structure construction
18 & 19   Digital construction models
   20   Centre Pompidou site plan

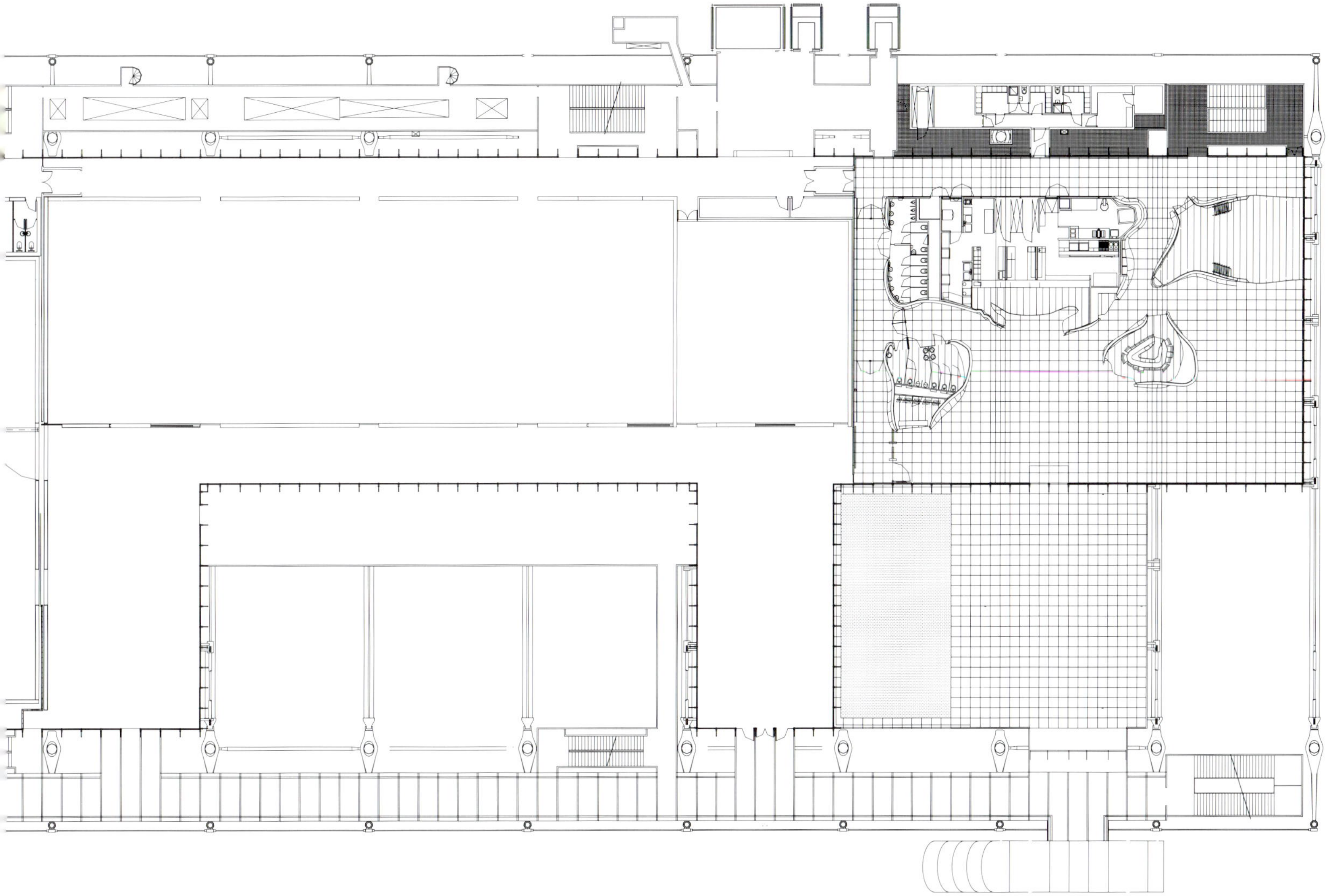

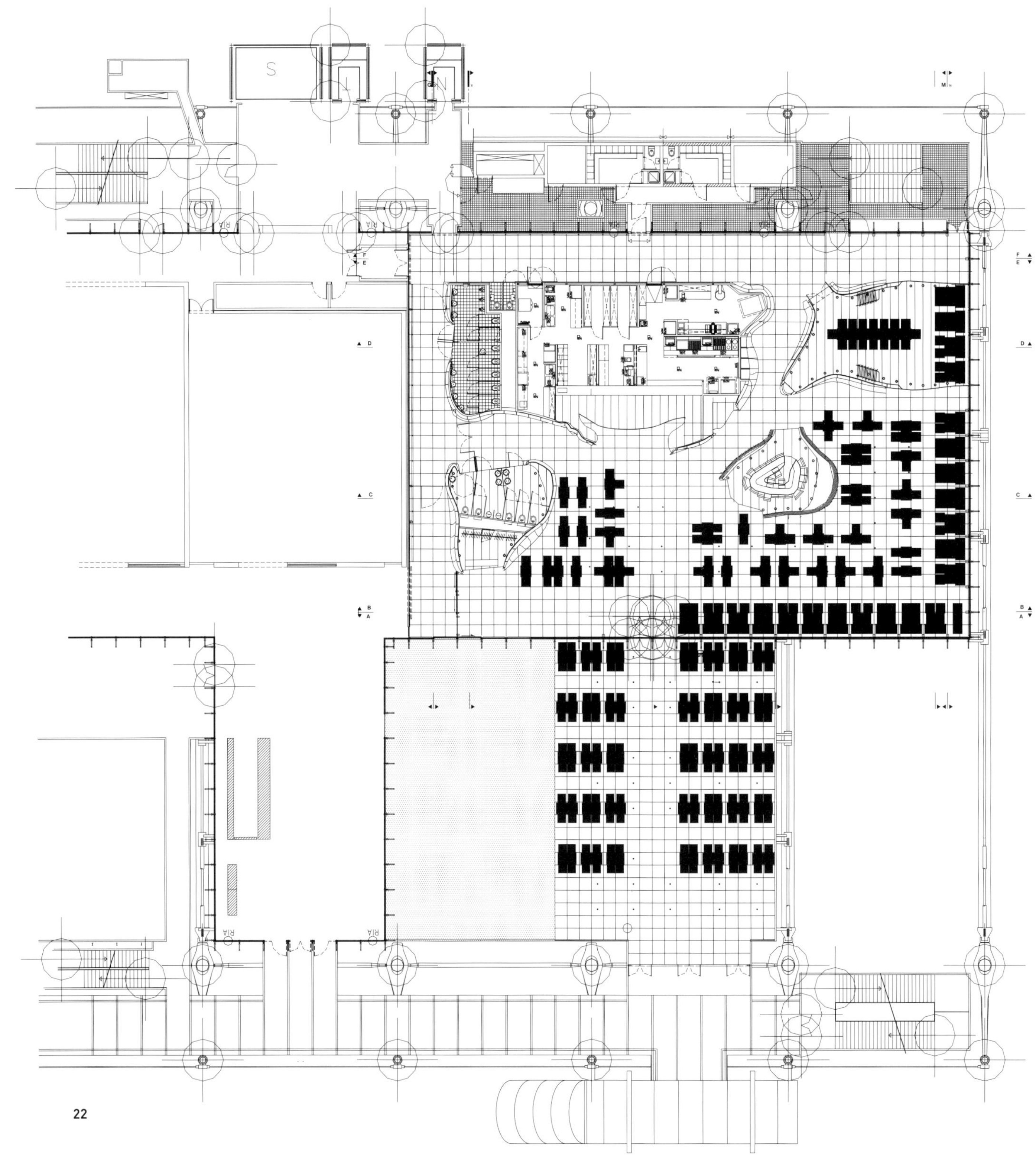

22   Plan of restaurant seating inside and outside terrace
23–26 Fabrication phase at shipyard

23

24

25

26

28

27

29

30

31

32

33

34

32 & 34   Red volume
     33   View from restaurant over Paris
     35   View of Pompidou showing red volume
     36   View between volumes at night

35

The client brief to our firm was to create a design for a bookshop that sells books created or conceptualised by artists. The nature of the store's holding is unique in France, similar in scope to the 'Printed Matter' bookstore in New York.

The brief was to create a shelving system for books using a miniscule floor area of 35 square metres. We decided to take the average-sized book as a planning and design increment, which would then define the dimensions of a shelving system into a 3D matrix of 360 mm x 360 mm x 360 mm. The matrix derived from this exercise established an infinite structural system that could fill the entire volume of the retail space.

In addition to this 3D solid matrix, we modelled an imaginary circulation route of a fictional customer, who through browsing, penetrates deeper into the solid matrix of the space. We found that this circulation route hollows out a good 70 percent of the solid crate.

When the circulation route was superimposed into the space of the shop, the result was three 'islands' of shelving, which were then in turn 'cored' to create the

necessary stock spaces on the inside of these volumes. What shapes the design of this project is the action of shopping and browsing, generating the solution to the shelving's final form. What is left over from this exercise is an ephemeral space: the book in this project has been utilised as an object of desire for browsing and purchase, as well as fabricator of its own architecture.

FLORENCE LOEWY BOOKSHOP

2001

Paris, France

JAKOB + MACFARLANE

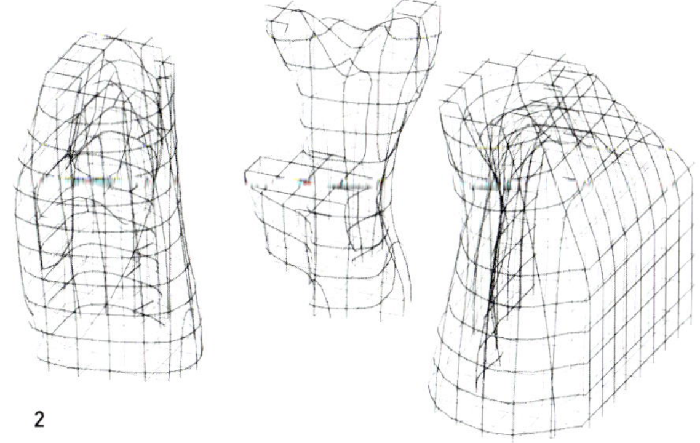

2

1 View of a book 'island'
2 Digital diagram of three 'islands'

1

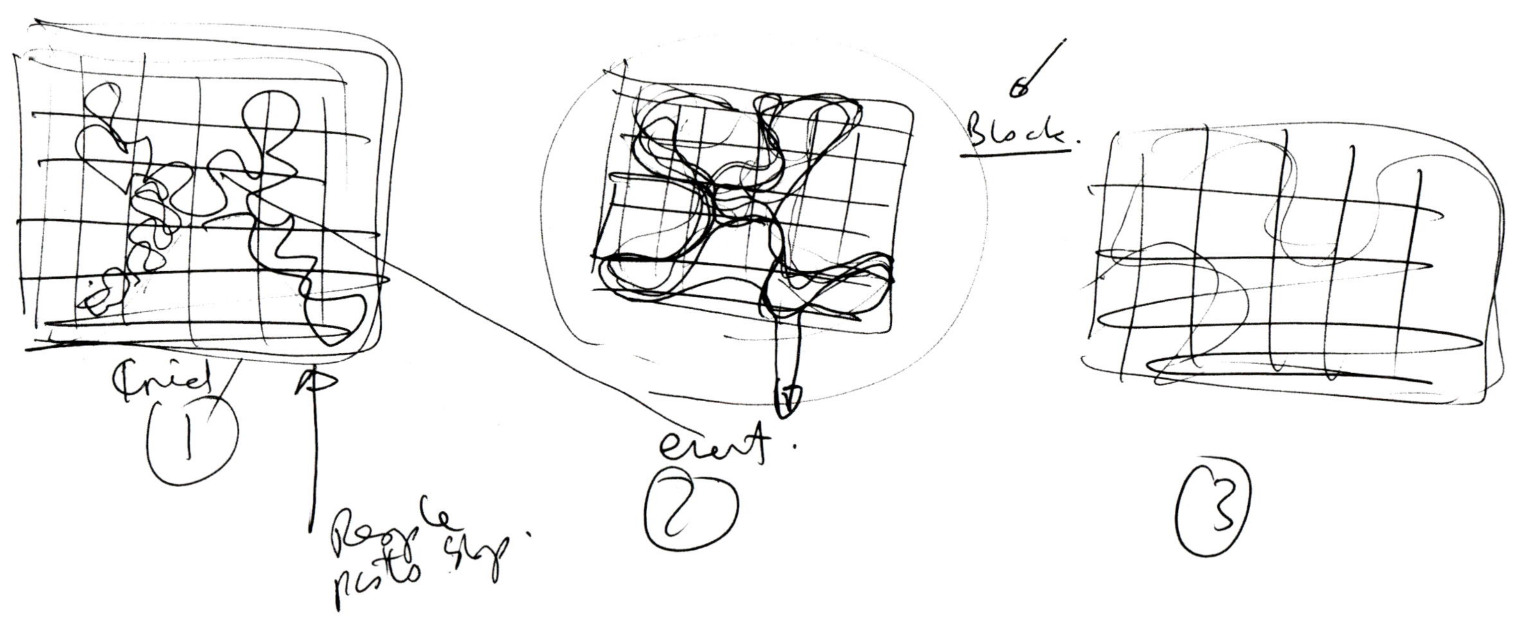

3

4

5

3   Conceptual sketches – showing path
    carving into matrix
4   Installation of prefabricated shelves
5   Digital model
6   View of three 'islands'
7   Books in place
Following pages:
    View from street looking through
    19th-century façade

7

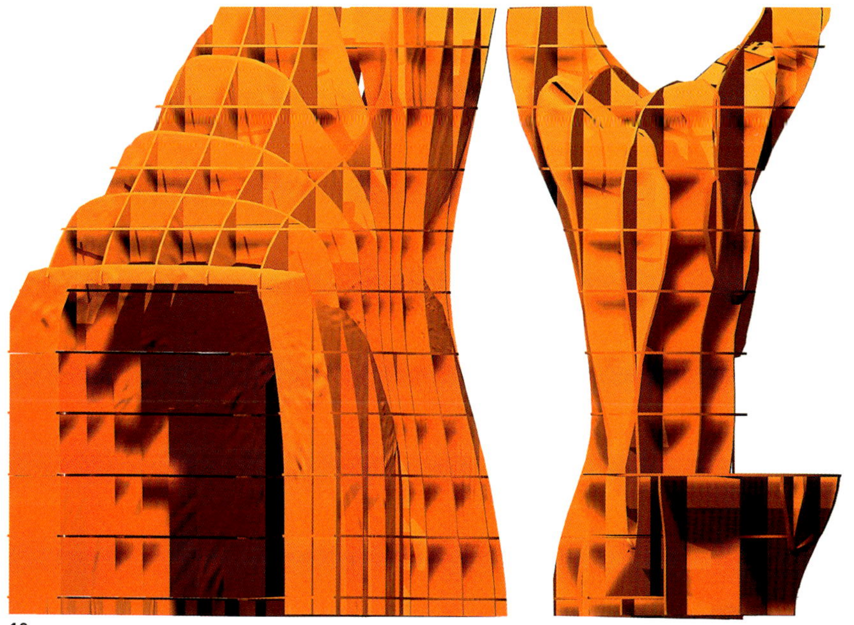

10

11

9 Shelf detail
10 Virtual model
11 Detail inside volume

JAKOB + MACFARLANE

House H is a private house commission on the island of Corsica, France. The house is designed around a dialogue between the topography of the site and the programme requirements of a residential dwelling. It is a house that unfolds over its site, the design responding to changes in climate, season and time of day.

Created digitally by modelling natural data, the house moulds around its terrain, with its cells opening and closing in accordance with different types of data input. For example helio-guidance: the movement of the sun or moon across the site; anemo-guidance: the direction of the wind (blowing in from the sea by day and from the direction of the mountains at night); and dèambulatoire-guidance or circulation (the movement of the human body moving through the house).

In realising the design of the project, a digital model of the site's topography was made and a surface cloned from an initial digital model was then superimposed over this model.

Elements of programme were then introduced between these two virtual surfaces. We then let these two layers seep into one another and deform like living shapes appropriating their environment. The result is a series of cellular spaces appearing on a surface guided by a 3D matrix of the topography.

1 & 2   Landscape site plans
3   View of house and landscape

HOUSE H

2001

Corsica, France

1

2

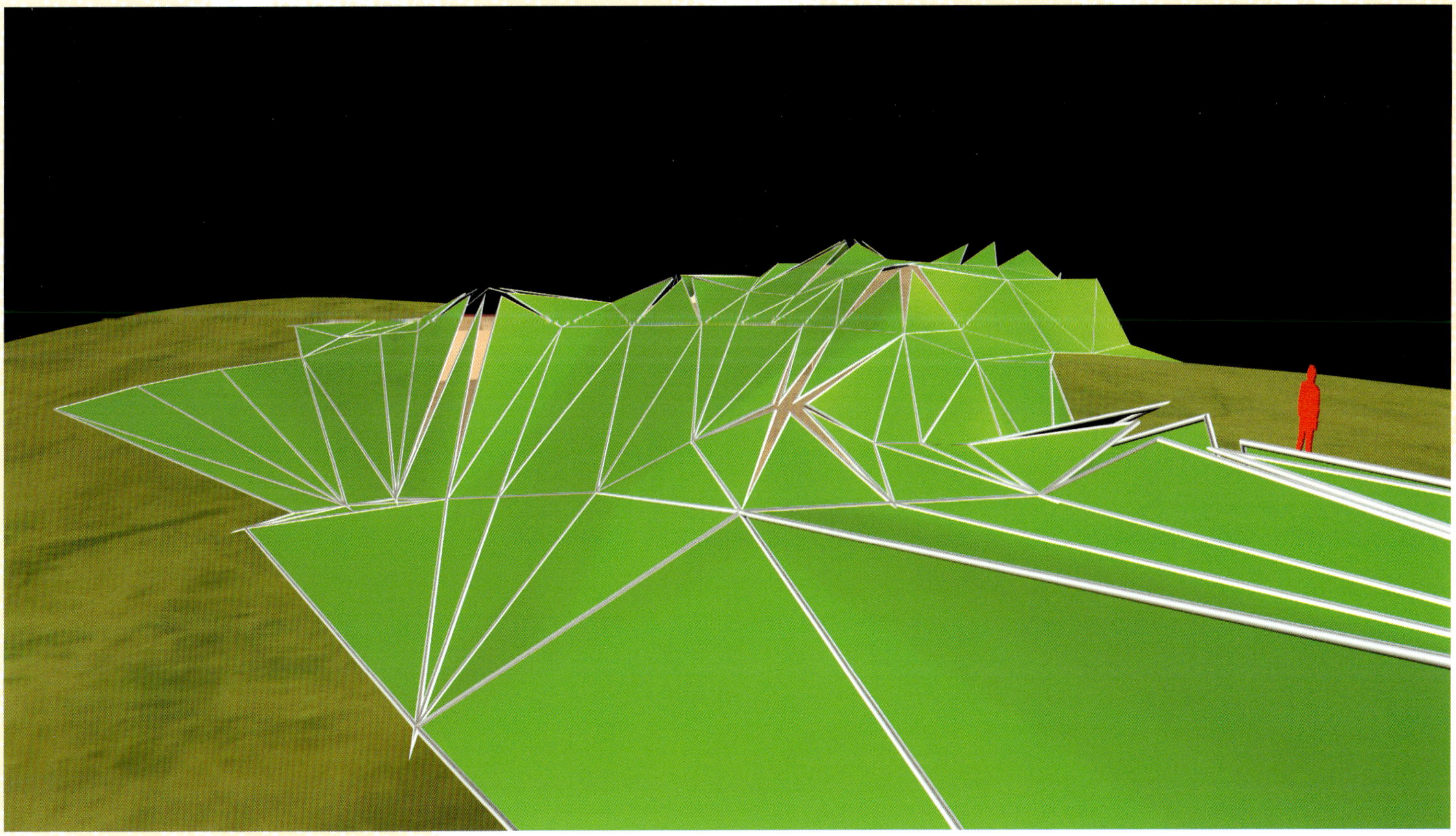

3

5

4

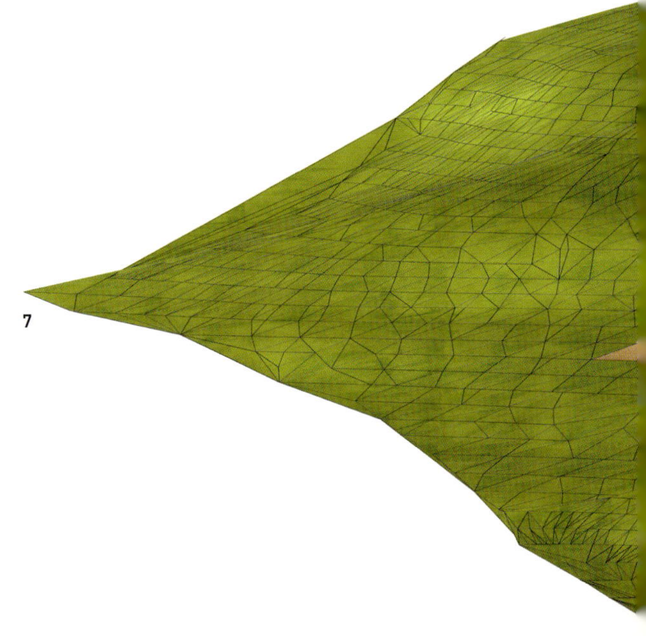

7

6

4–6 Views of site
7 Study view of complete site with different program elements
8 View inside bush scrub on site

8

9

10

11

12

13

9 & 10   Views of site
11   Digital modelling – topographic lattice
12 & 13   Digital studies
14   Roof surface openings study

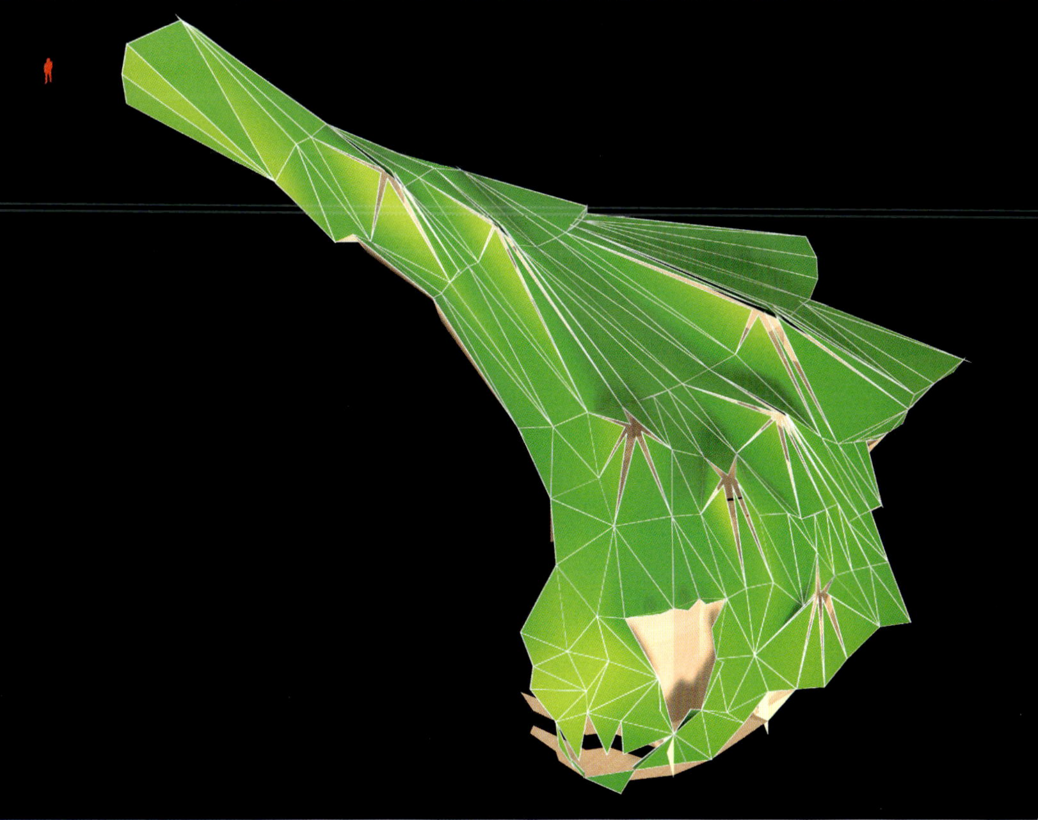

14

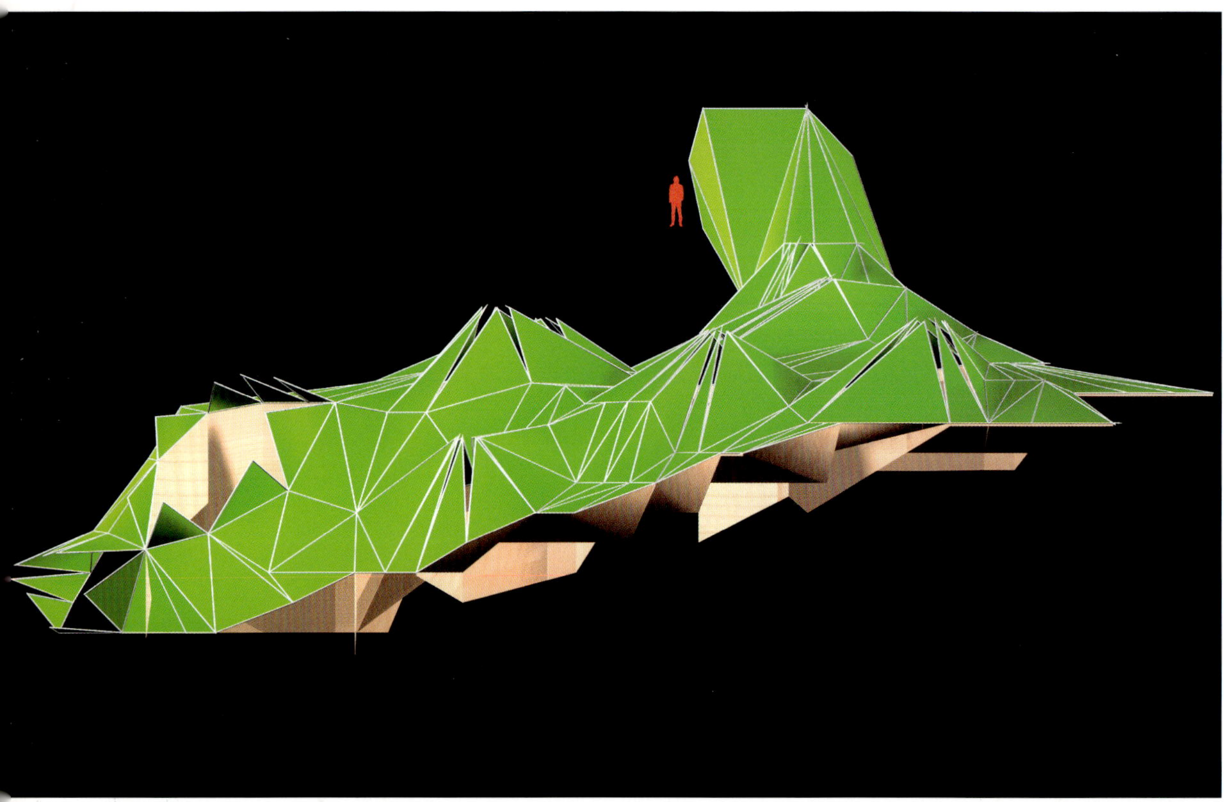

15

17

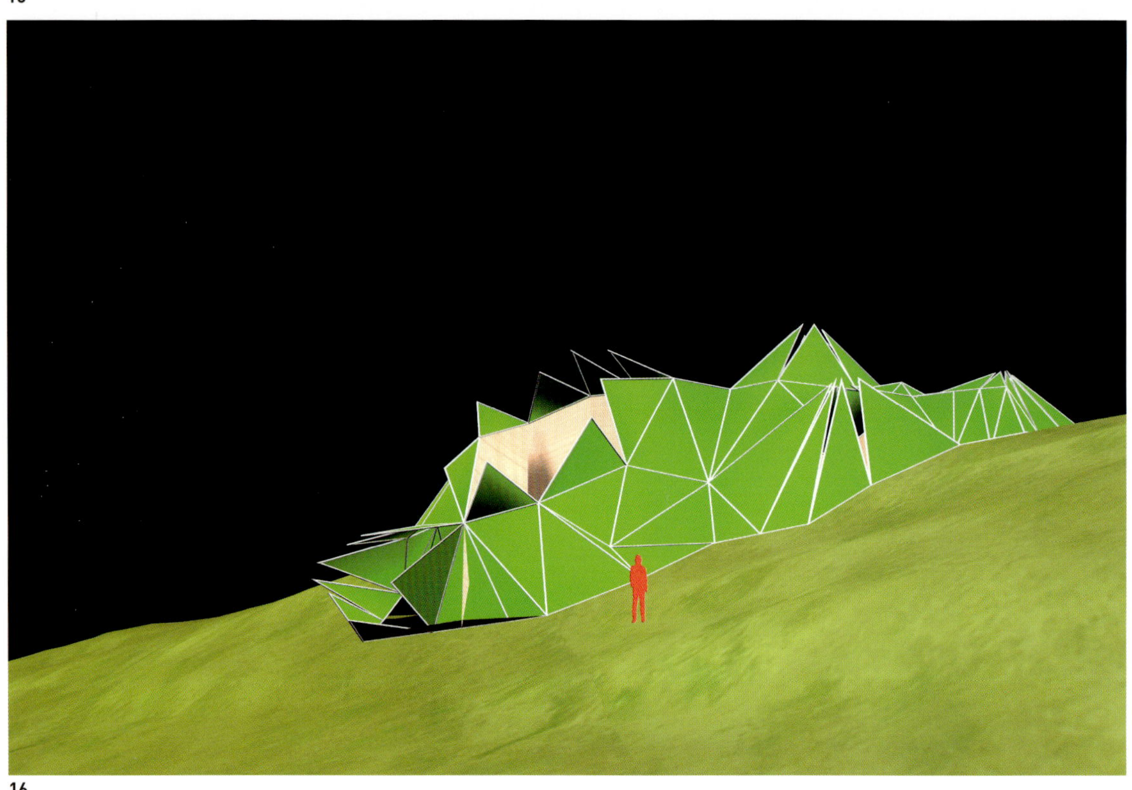

16

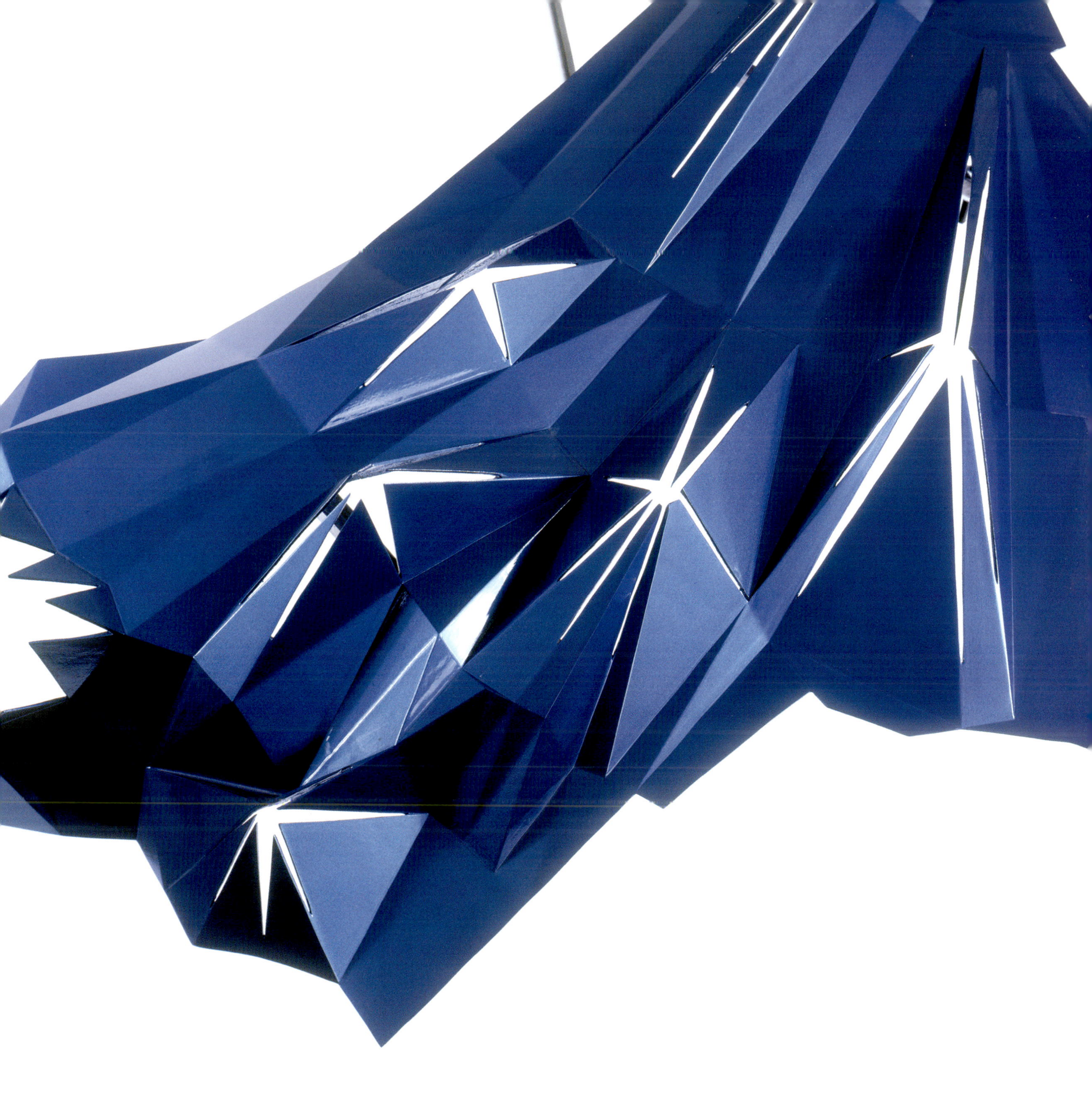

15 & 16   Digital studies of house outside and inside site – Collection Frac. Orleans
17   Mould model of digital study – Collection Frac. Orleans

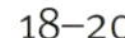

18

19

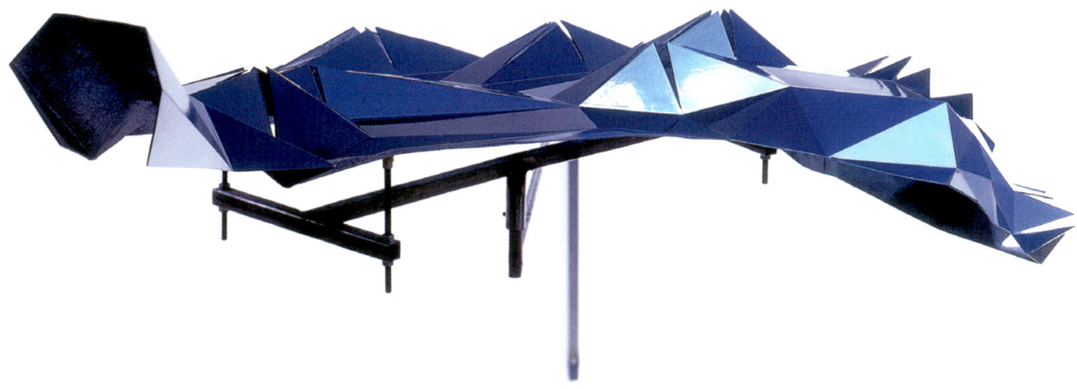

20

We desire to express grief over what happened on this site. At the same time, we feel that the very nature of a 'New World Trade Center', without addressing some of the most pressing issues of our time, is absurd. How can one talk of trade on this site now? Surely the issues and the questions this site raises are deeper, and the level of responsibility more substantial than mere trade.

We propose a project that would deal with remembering, as well as with global issues. What could come from this great loss that would help rekindle hope and faith across the world?

This site now belongs to the world.

We need to think peace.

Our project proposes a series of towers, or long thin 'fingers'. The spirit is light and sensual, healing and responsive. These towers would act as huge signals or light messages symbolising issues that we feel are compelling to this traumatic event and the times in which we live.

1   Model of the project as exhibited in the French pavilion at the 8th Bienale of Venice, 2002
2   Digital model – plan view

A NEW WORLD PEACE CENTER

Invitation project, 2002

New York City, USA

1

2

3   Digital model – elevation
4   Digital model – plan view
5   Model of the project as exhibited in the French pavilion at the 8th
    Bienale of Venice, 2002
6   View of project from New York Harbor, inserted into World Trade
    tower site

4

3

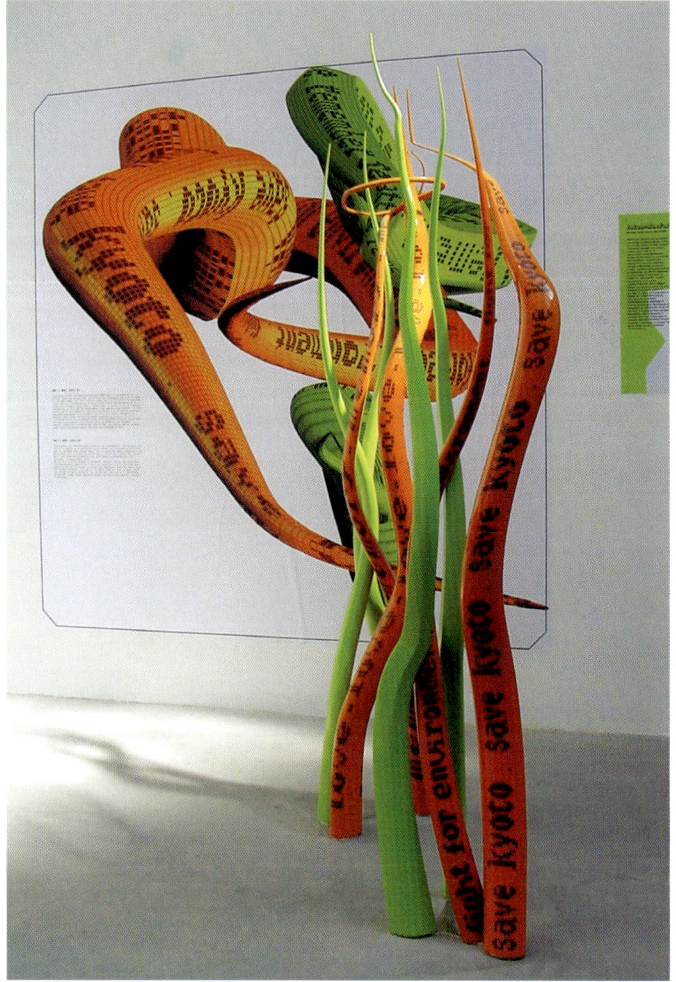

5

save the environment
remember

Renault's requirement, as outlined in the brief for this project, was to create a series of spaces for exhibitions, conferences, office space and general corporate activity in connection with public relations.

Rather than starting the planning and design from scratch on a greenfield site, our firm was asked to convert an existing industrial building that was completed in the early 1980s by Claude Vasconi. This building was the last remaining structure of what had once been the huge Renault industrial car complex at Boulogne-Billancourt, before Renault decentralised its operations in the early 1980s.

The design and planning of the project was intended to realise a space that could clearly be perceived as a new insertion within the existing building envelope, but in such a way that it would also achieve a spatial and functional dialogue with the existing context.

By utilising the existing geometry of the repeating industrial roofline of the Vasconi building, which when seen in section recreates the Renault logo, we proposed a series of planes conceptually extruded downwards, which directly relate back to the existing industrial roof structure. Through this process, a field of white walls was created which came to define our new intervention along an east–west axis. Secondary timber walls defined and completed these volumes along a north–south axis. This new field of walls and associated enclosed volumes became the solution to reappropriating the existing space: a field of walls, which respond to and are directly informed by the functional demands of the brief.

The design/planning solution allows for complete autonomy between the different functional aspects of the program, while at the same time structurally creating the largest possible open-plan exhibition space on the ground floor. A large part of the remaining required functions are suspended above the ground floor, creating a huge viewing promenade and achieving a visual interlinking of the various elements in the brief.

The principal programme elements are three amphitheatres (300, 500 and 100 seats), three seminar rooms, a press room, four large open-plan office spaces, a garage for 36 cars, a private meeting area, storerooms, a kitchen and ancillary spaces totalling more than 14,000 square metres.

The original interior finishes of the existing steel structure and ceilings were restored in order to clearly reinforce the dialogue between the existing structure and the new insertions. Externally, a huge glass roof creates a new entrance space located between two existing buildings. On the eastern side of the existing exterior, a new steel and glass façade will eventually face the new urban square to connect this project with the future projects of the Ile Seguin development area.

1 & 2   Factory space before architectural insertion
3   View from east façade looking into vast exhibition space

RENAULT WORLD COMMUNICATION CENTER

2005

Boulogne-Billancourt, France

3

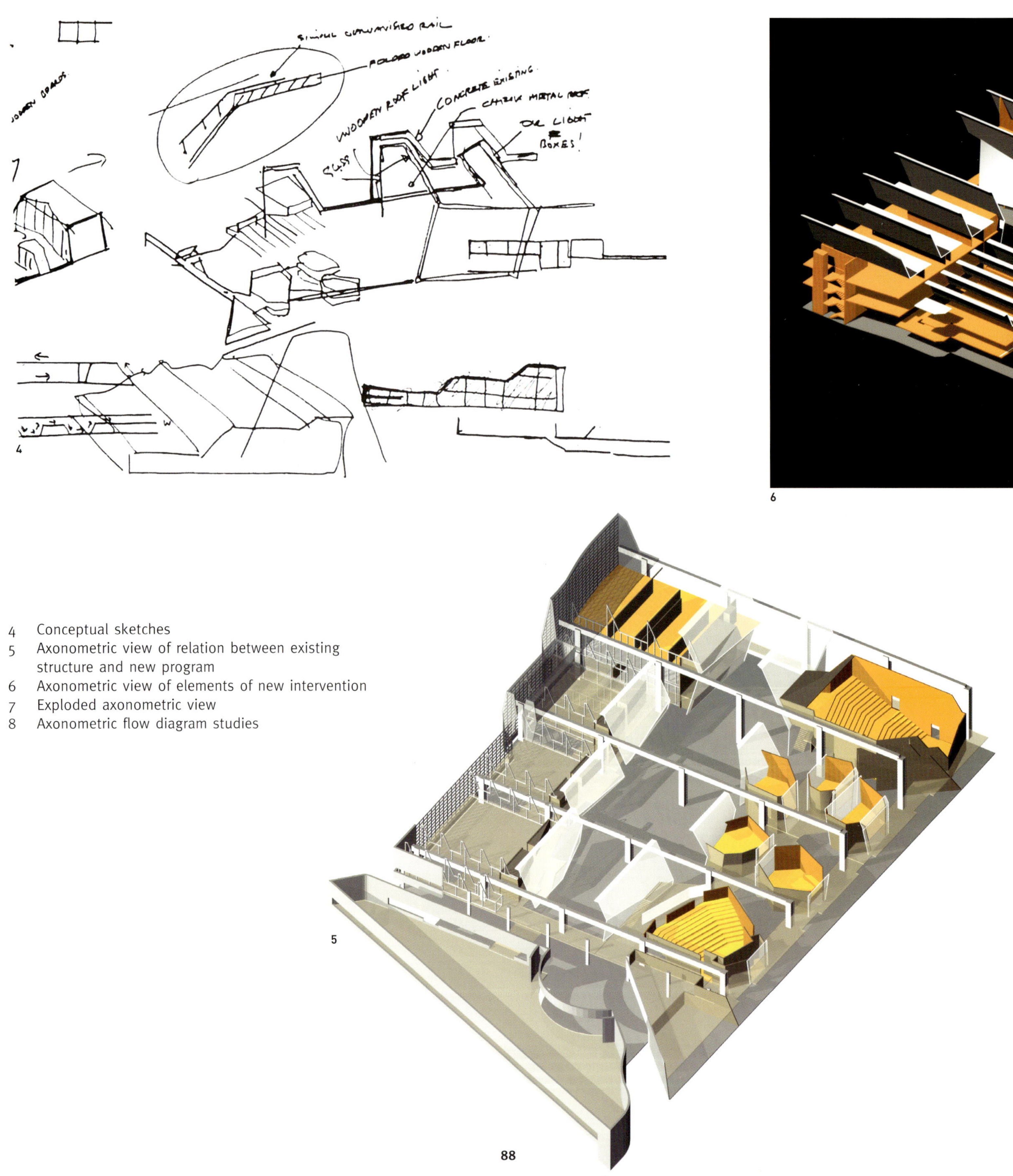

4 Conceptual sketches
5 Axonometric view of relation between existing
   structure and new program
6 Axonometric view of elements of new intervention
7 Exploded axonometric view
8 Axonometric flow diagram studies

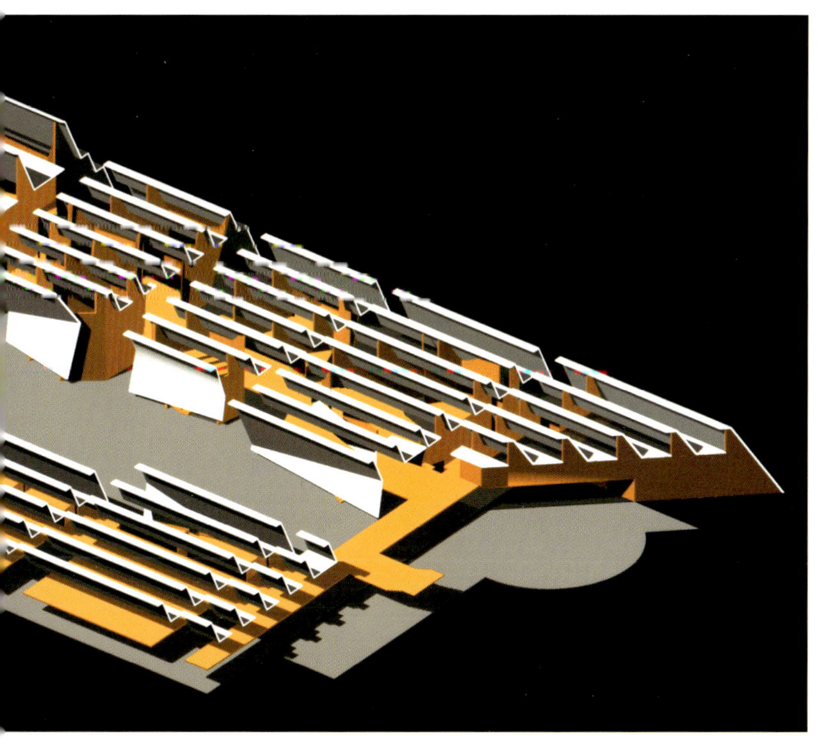

7

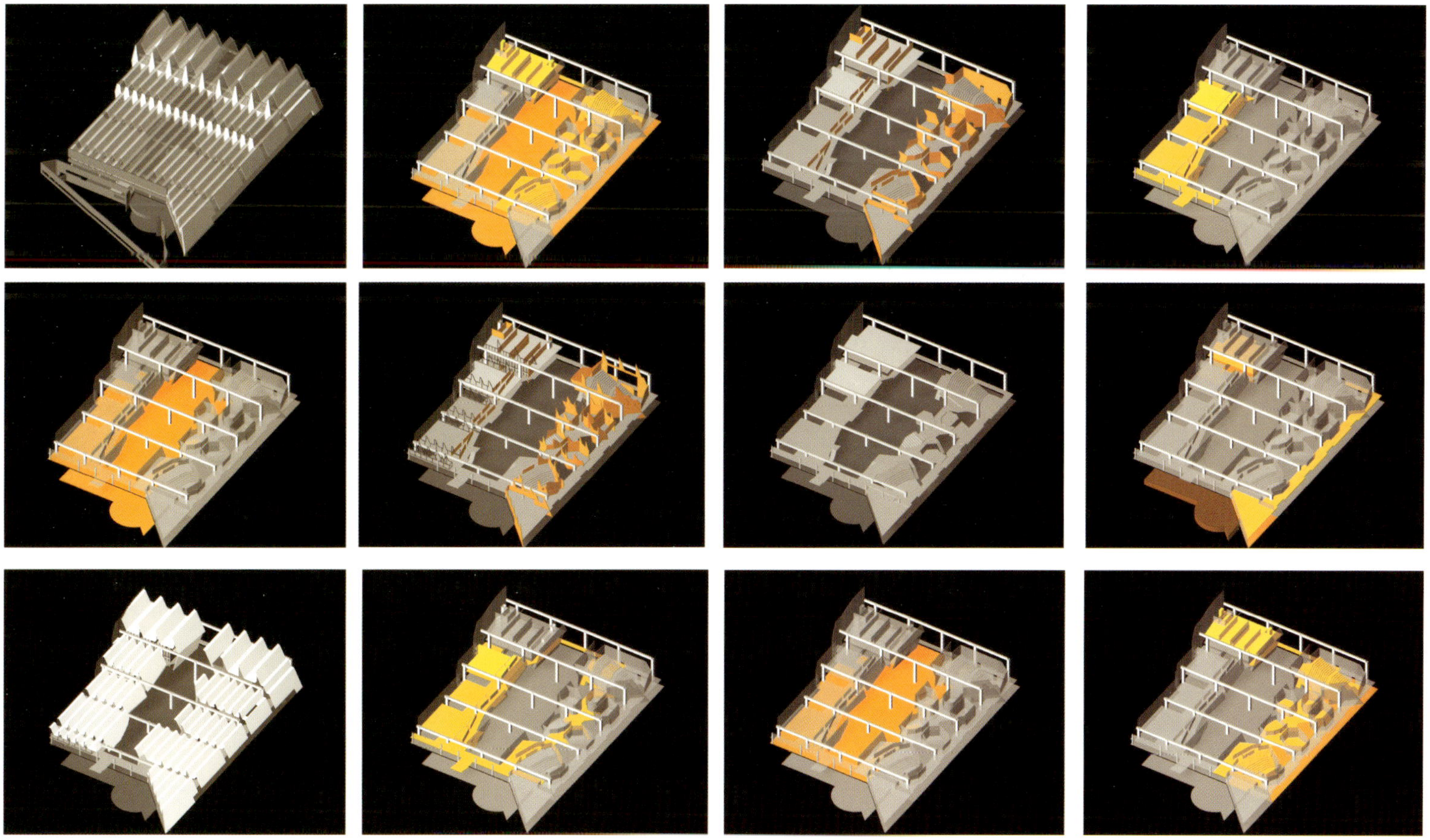

8

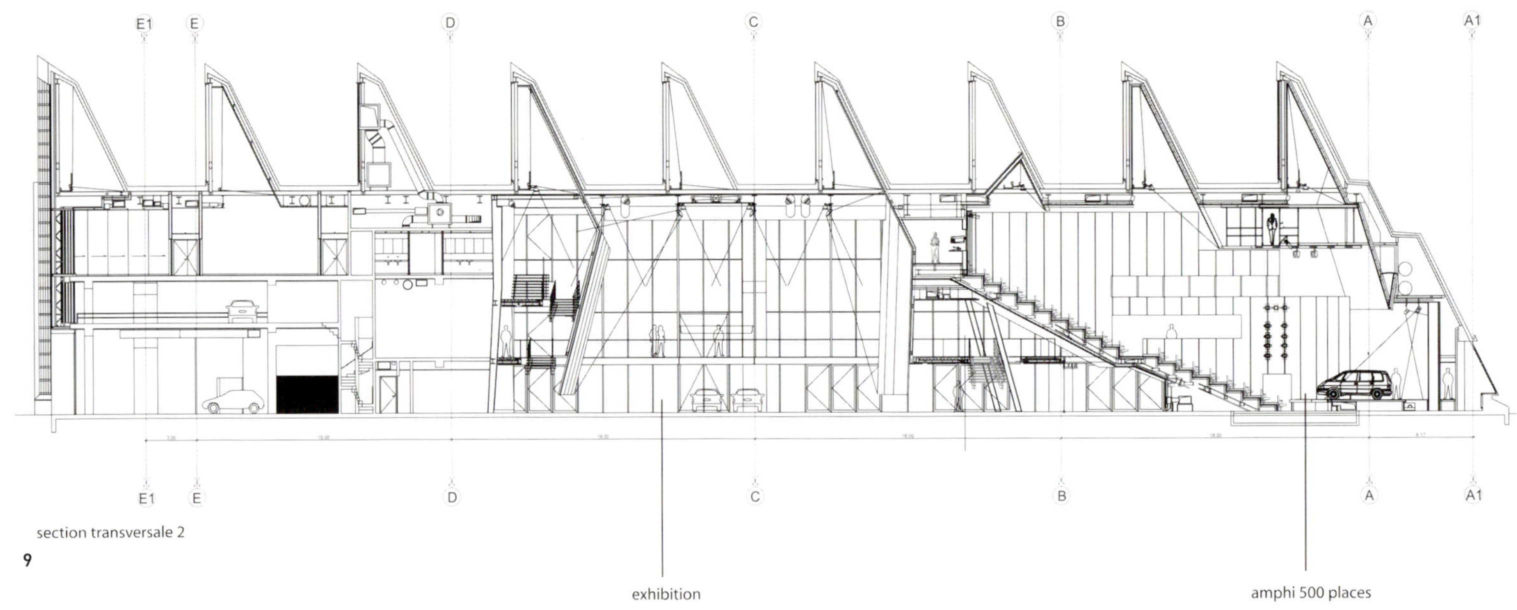

10

9   Transversal section through 500-person amphitheatre and garage
10 View showing existing buildings with new interior intervention
11 Meeting place between different volumes

12

13

14

12	View of main exhibition space
13	View of aluminium pleated wall descending from roof light
14	Detail view under mezzanine showing stair looking towards main exhibition space
15	View of light walls and volumes behind
16	Oak panelling with white walls in honeycomb aluminium

17

18

19

17 View of mezzanine level
18 Unfinished office space
19 Light walls
20 Meeting room

21 View behind a light wall
22 Meeting place
23 100-seat theatre with rotating car floor
24 Meeting room

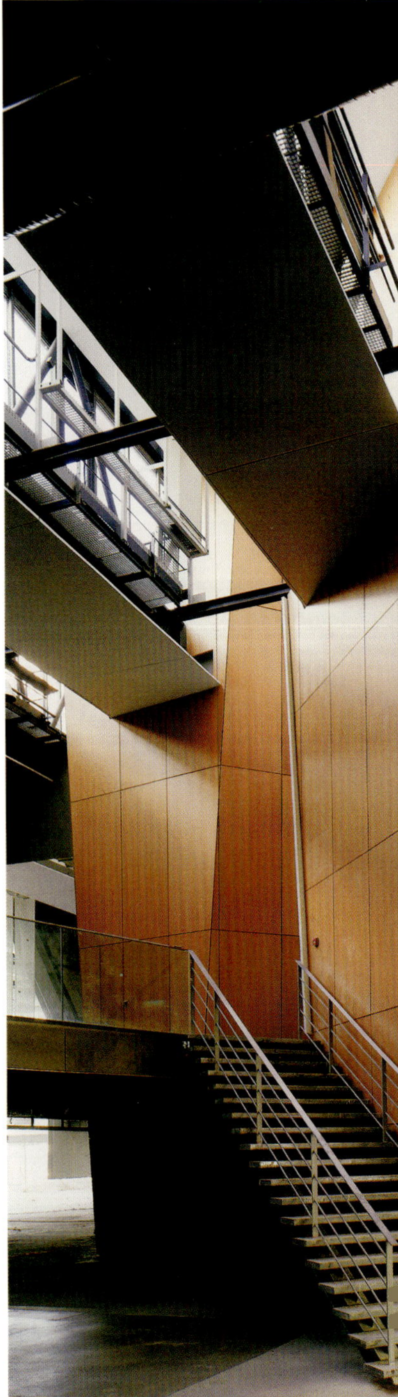

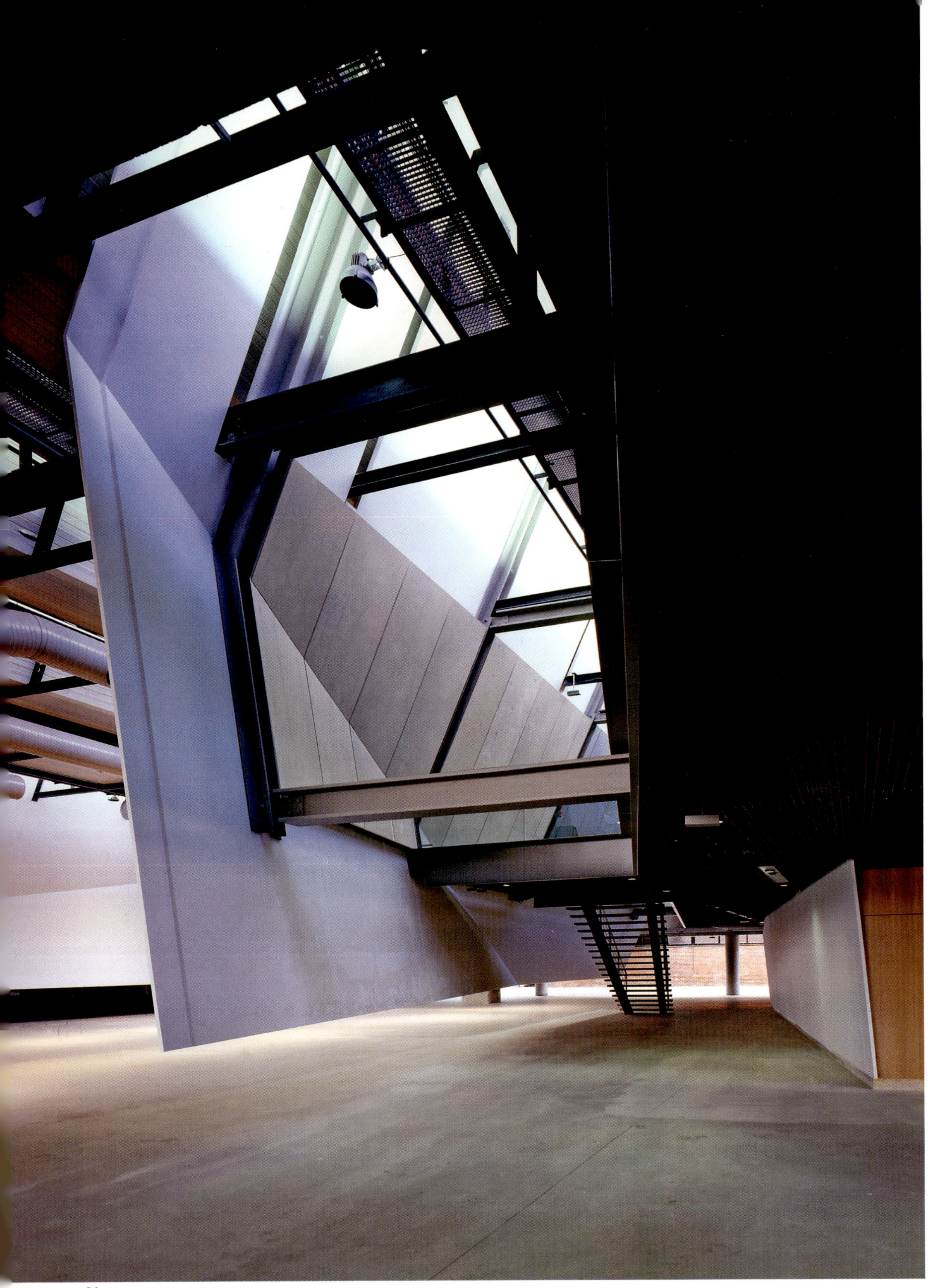

21

22

23

24

The programme set by the client for the 100 Apartments project calls for the design of apartments of varying size, with the ground floor being reserved to accommodate apartments for handicapped people. In addition to this programme, the relatively straightforward brief requested a series of shops at street level.

The site planning involved the creation of three separate buildings on fragments of the existing site. The fragmentation of the site resulted from various factors such as site views, Hausmanian setback rules, the preservation of old-growth trees and a stringent site development code.

After studying the requirements for development and the difficulty they imposed, we decided to conceive of the buildings in a way that accentuates the existing urban condition and that of the site, creating a relation between the site and its developmental limitations.

The project is conceived as a large-scale urban 3D matrix, to which we applied a careful 'cutting' and 'coring' process. The finished project is a result of both existing urban and ecological factors, which register as conceptual starting points and determining factors in the creation of the design of new urban space.

1

100 APARTMENTS

2006

Paris, France

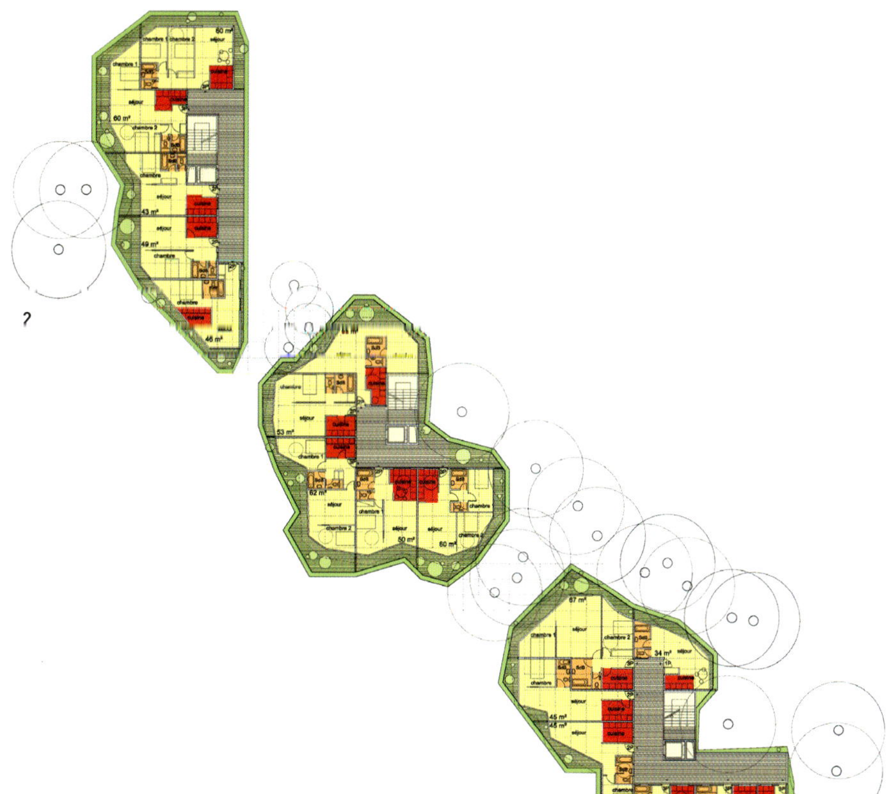

1   View of apartments from communal gardens
2   General plan

Rue du Général Brunet
Boulevard Serrurier
Rue Francis Ponge
E.V.I.P
4501 m²
Limite de l'EVIP
Entrée Bâtiment A
Emprise Hall sur boulevard
[local poubelles- vélos...]   45 m²
+78.10 NGF
Entrée Bâtiment B
Emprise Hall sur boulevard
[local poubelles- vélos...]   43 m²
+79.70 NGF
Entrée Bâtiment C
+84.50 NGF
+85.50
Accès Parkings
Accès Parkings
A
B
C
64 m²
chambre 1   chambre 2   séjour
chambre 2   cuisine
séjour   cuisine
70 m²   chambre 1
SdB
chambre
séjour   cuisine
42 m²
49 m²   cuisine
séjour
chambre
SdB
SdB
chambre
cuisine
49 m²
chambre
séjour   SdB
52 m²   cuisine
SdB   cuisine   cuisine   SdB
séjour   séjour   séjour
39 m²   chambre 1   50 m²   60 m²   chambre 2
chambre
séjour   SdB
46 m²   cuisine
chambre   SdB
45 m²   cuisine
séjour
chambre
cuisine   séjour
44 m²   chambre
SdB
local vélo
poubelles
SdB   cuisine   cuisine
chambre   séjour   séjour   SdB   séjour
chambre 2   60 m²   chambre   70 m²   chambre 2   66 m²   chambre 2
chambre 1

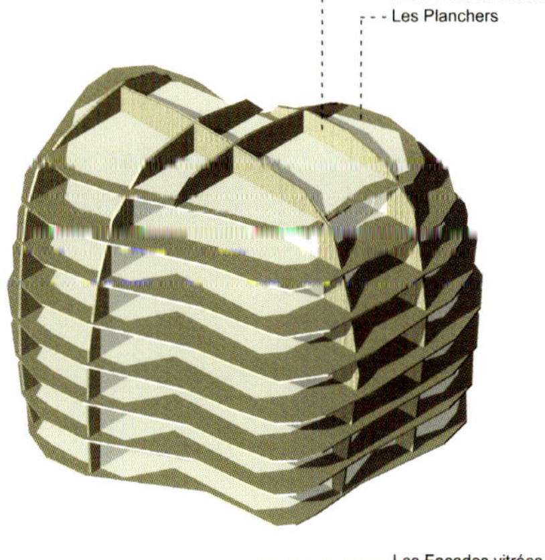

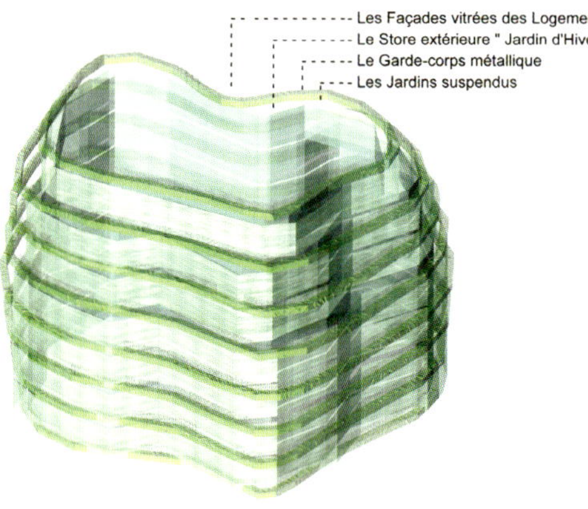

3   Ground floor plan
4   View from street
5   Axonometric structure and skin studies

The city of Saint-Nazaire and its train station were heavily damaged by bombing in World War II, leaving the train station site and surrounds ripe for considerable redevelopment in post-war years. The Le Fanal National Theatre complex was a project commissioned to create a performance theatre and an adjoining rehearsal theatre annex on the footprint of the destroyed Saint-Nazaire train station.

Our approach to this project was to use the existing, but heavily damaged, building grid of 4.5 x 4.5 metres. From this, a new conceptual grid was produced that is extruded upwards and downwards to different heights in order to meet the different functional and spatial needs of the respective components of the theatre's programme. The result is the realisation of a new kind of extruded topographic language consisting of opaque and transparent elements.

The design of extruded topographies on the site creates a new urbanscape as viewed in the context of the town's built environment, as well as recalling metaphorical readings of voyages, container ships and shipyards, and other industrial paraphernalia associated with the City of Saint-Nazaire.

The programme for the complex is separated into three essential parts: a main theatre, a rehearsal theatre annex and artists' dressing rooms with administration facilities. In addition to these three central functional requirements, the theatre complex also houses an exhibition hall as part of the main entrance foyer, in addition to a café and a workshop.

The intention was that the interior single space of the complex be experienced in two ways. The interior volume can be either fully open between the stage and auditorium – this is what we have termed 'the storm', or stage-auditorium space – or, the space can be divided and closed off to create a more intimate, separated spatial experience. Visually, the interior of the Le Fanal Theatre complex has been designed to present its technical environment utilising this aesthetic, but realised in a simple stripped-back manner in order to not interfere with the experience of the theatre and its activities when in use.

LE FANAL NATIONAL THEATRE AT SAINT-NAZAIRE

2006

City of Saint-Nazaire, France

1

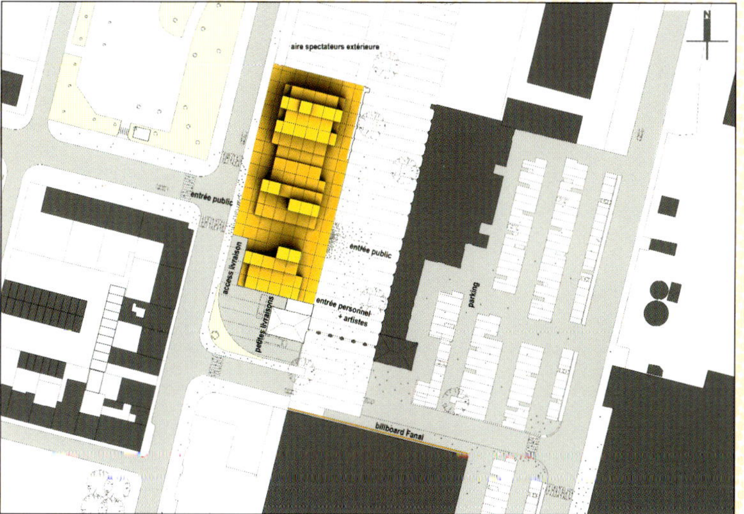

2

1 Axonometric view showing new project
  inserted into remnants of old train station
2 Site plan

F A N A L
tête
corps
flux des techniciens
flux des artistes
flux du public
flux de l'administratif
flux des livraisons
flux du secours
Axonométrie éclatée

3

4

Répétition

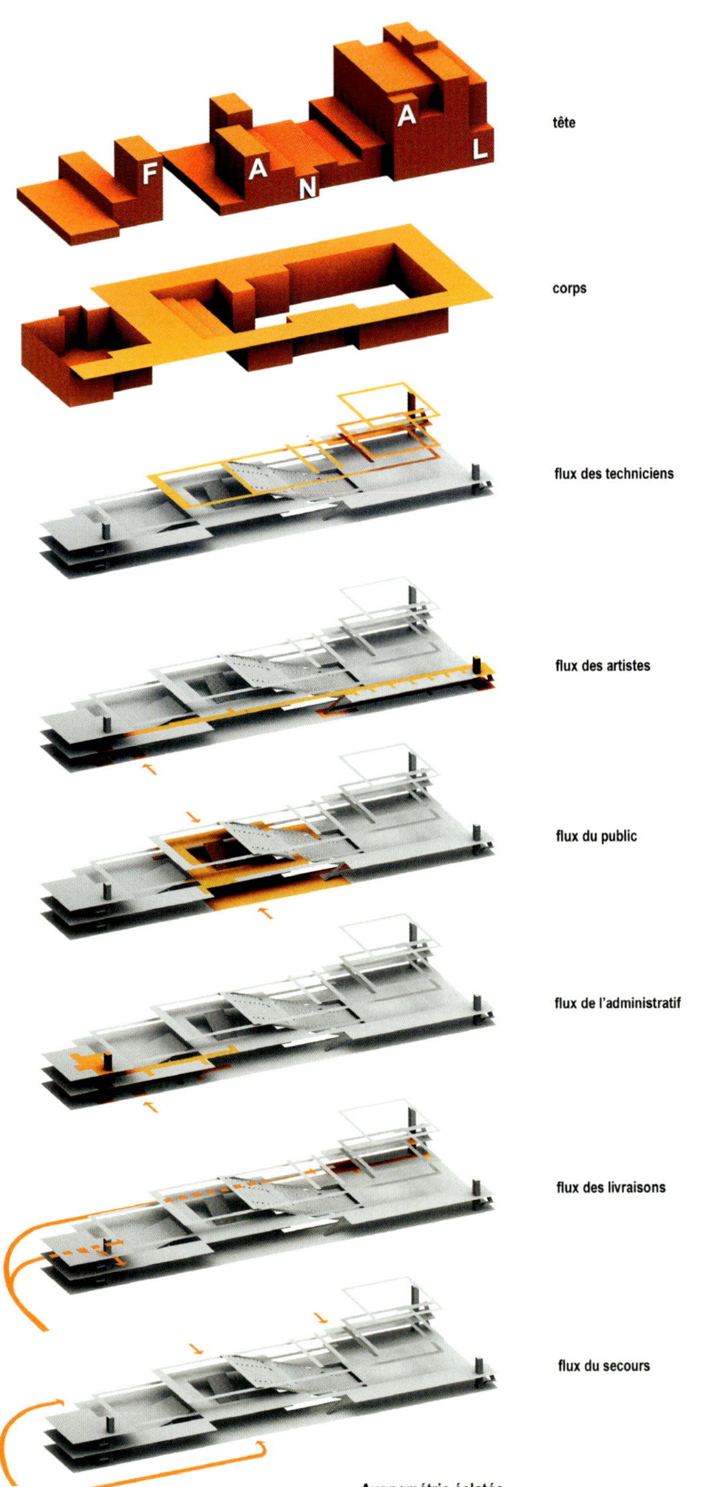

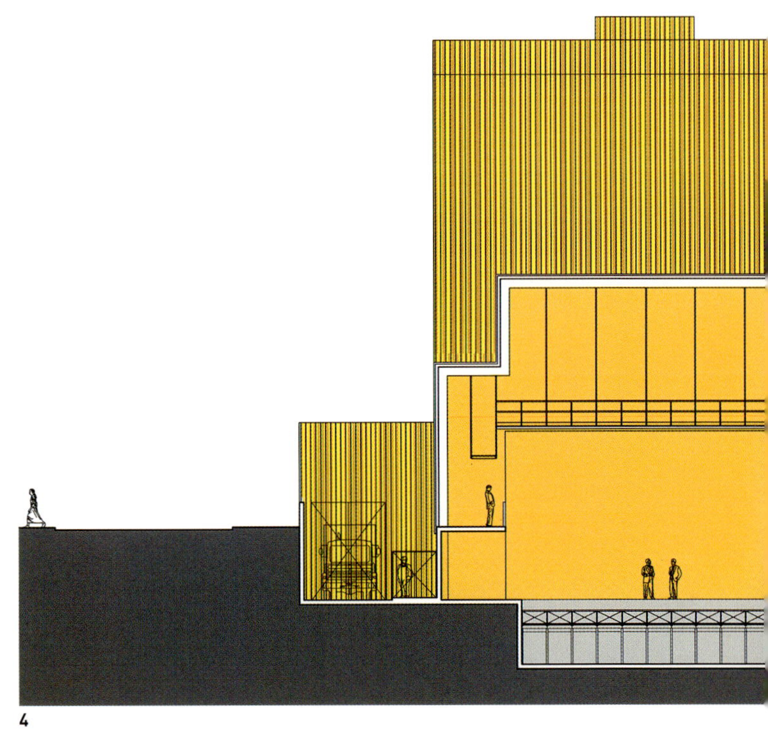

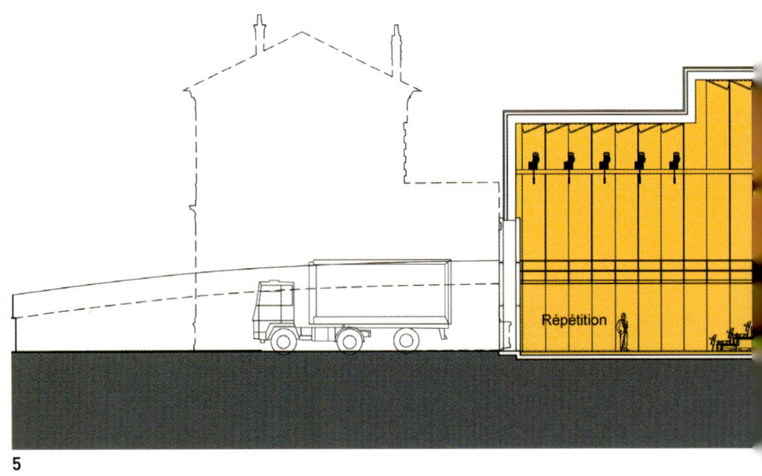

5

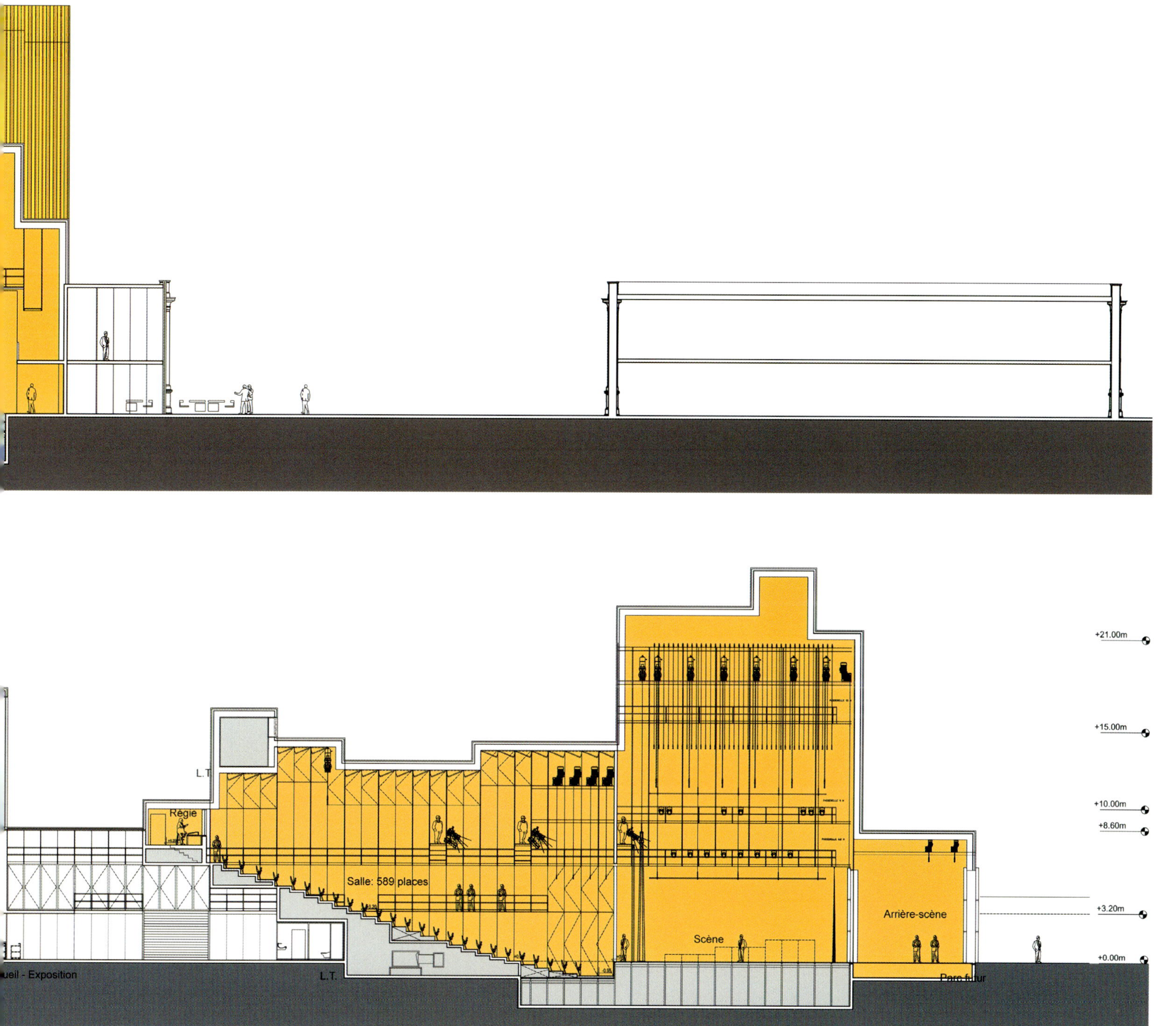
L.T.
Régie
Salle: 589 places
Scène
Arrière-scène
Accueil - Exposition
L.T.
Paroi futur
+21.00m
+15.00m
+10.00m
+8.60m
+3.20m
+0.00m

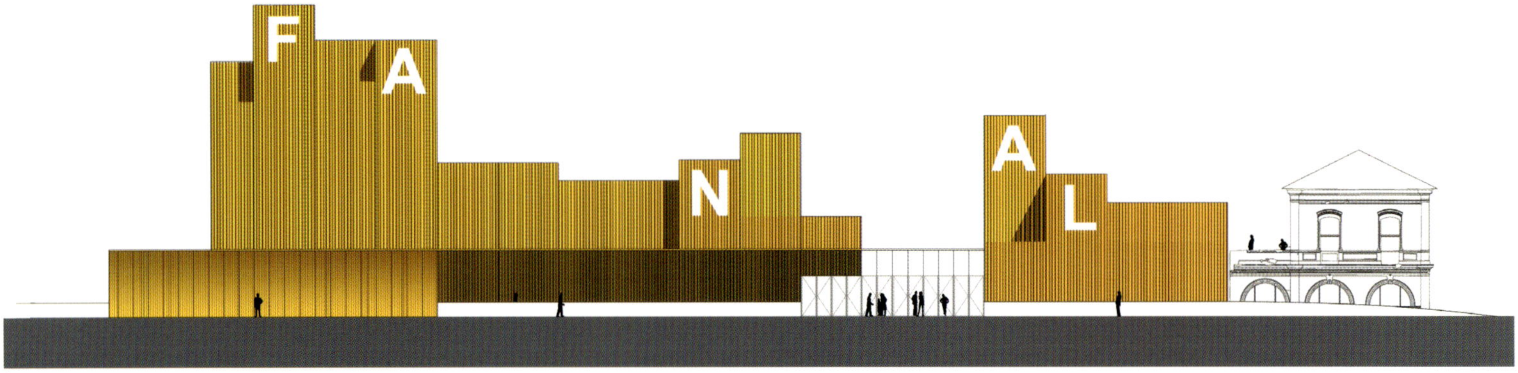

6   Elevation of theatre complex from the west
7   Elevation of theatre complex from the east
8   Perspective view from inside old train station central space

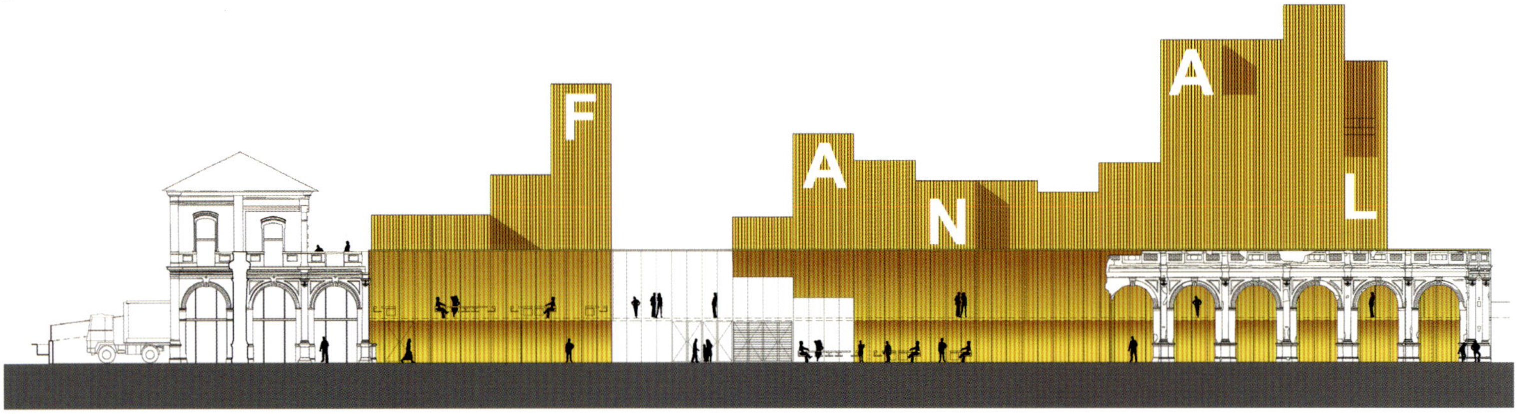

F
A
N
A
L

9

9   Main theatre auditorium with opening from stage onto adjacent garden
10   View of the entrance hall/foyer of the complex

The Docks of Paris is a long, thin building built in concrete at the turn of the last century. It was a depot for goods brought up the Seine by barge, which were deposited, and then transferred to dray or train.

The city of Paris launched a competition to create a new cultural program and building on this site. Whether or not to incorporate the existing concrete structure was a choice left to the participants.

Jakob+MacFarlane opted to retain the existing structure and use it to form and influence the new project. The concept of the new programme was known as a 'Plug-Over'. Here, the idea was to create a new external skin that both protects the existing structure and forms a new layer containing most of the public circulation systems and added program, as well as creating a new top floor to the existing building.

The new structural system supporting this skin is the result of a systematic deformation of the existing conceptual grid of the docks building. A tree-like generating method is used to create a new system from the existing system, that is, 'growing' the new building from the old as new branches grow on a tree.

This skin is created principally from a glass exterior skin, steel structure, wood decking and a prairie-faceted roofscape.

The 'Plug-Over' operates not only as a way of exploiting the maximum building envelope but enables a continuous public path to move up through the building from the lowest level alongside the Seine to the roof deck and back down, a kind of continuous loop enabling the building to become part of the urban condition.

The programme is a rich mix centred around the themes of design and fashion, including exhibition spaces, a French fashion institute, music producers, bookshops, cafés and a restaurant.

1

THE DOCKS OF PARIS

2006

Paris, France

1 Night view from the Seine
2 View from public roof deck and view over the Seine

3   Transversal section through surrounding urban condition showing 'plug over'
4   Elevation from river
5   Axonometric study of existing structure and new skin
6   Axonometric study of programmatic elements

3

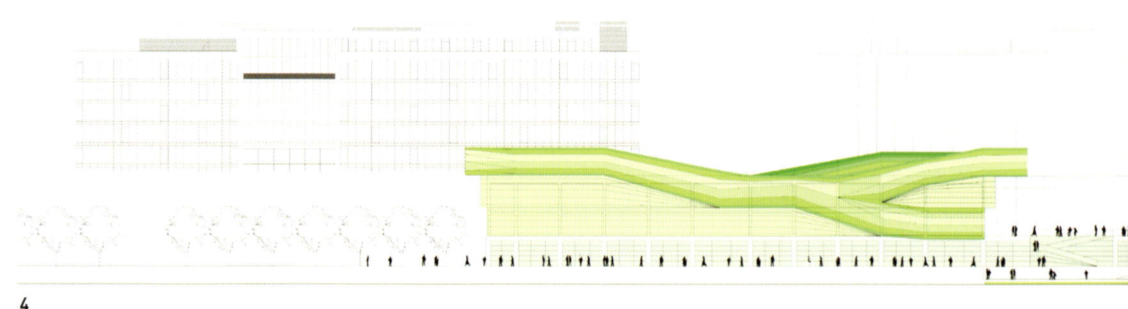

4

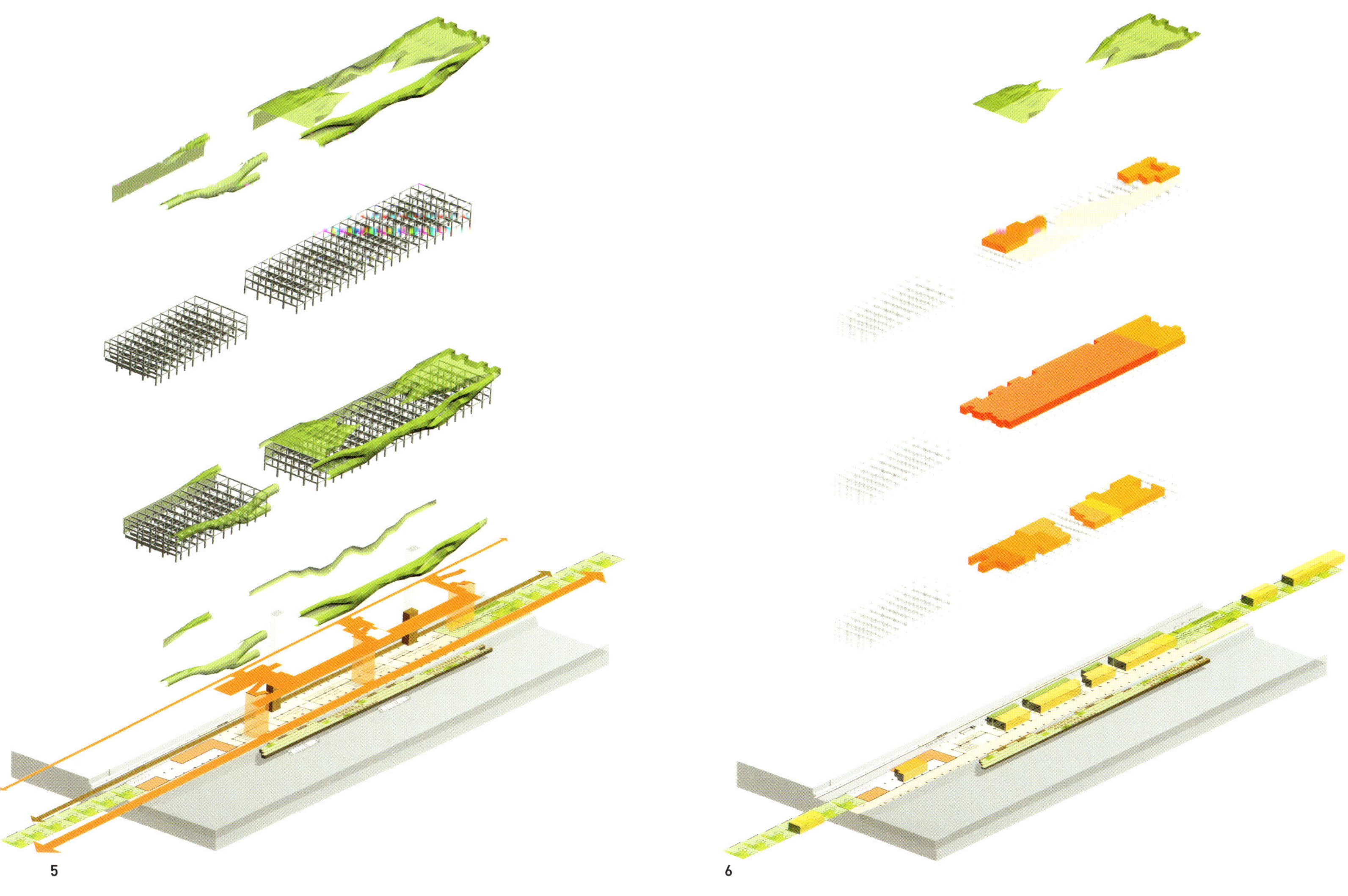

5

6

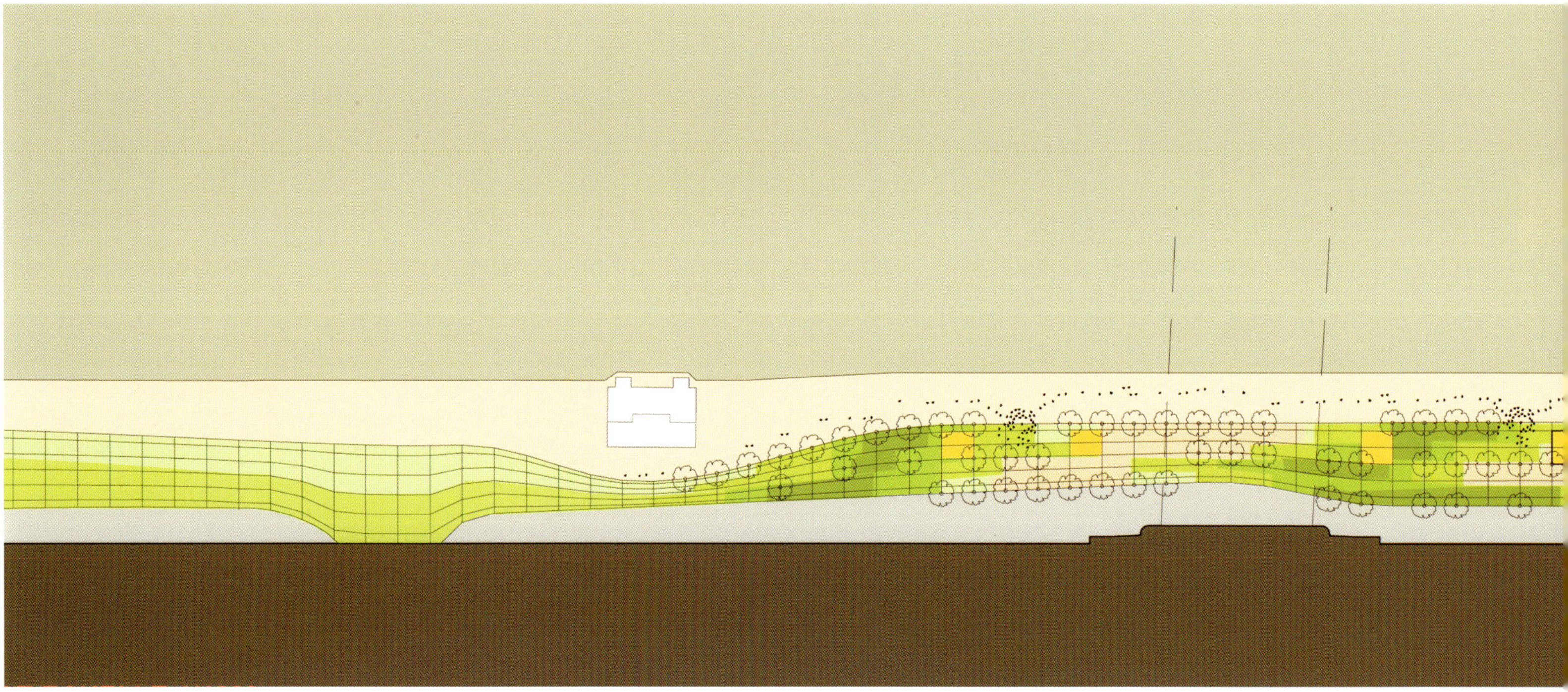

7

7 Plan at quay level
8 View of main entry space
9 Perspective view of 'plug over' with floating terrace and boat deck

8

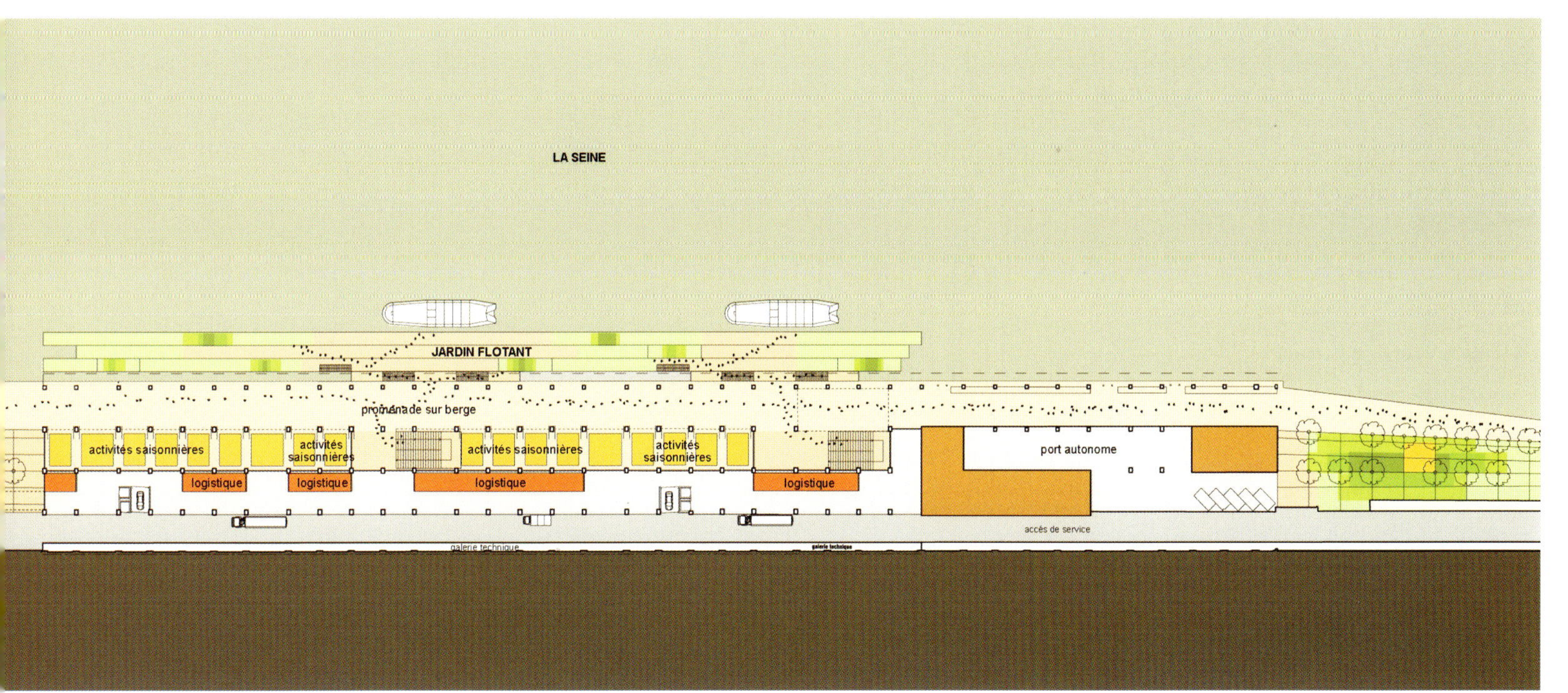
LA SEINE
JARDIN FLOTANT
promenade sur berge
activités saisonnières
activités saisonnières
activités saisonnières
activités saisonnières
logistique
logistique
logistique
logistique
port autonome
accès de service
galerie technique
galerie technique

Jakob+MacFarlane is an architectural firm based in Paris, France. Its work explores digital technology both as a conceptual consideration and as a means of fabrication, using new materials as a possibility to create a more flexible, responsive and immediate environment.

Main projects to date include the T House at la Garenne Colombes, Paris, France (1998), Restaurant Georges at the Georges Pompidou Centre, Paris (2000) and the reconstruction of the Theatre of Pont-Audemer, France (1999–2000). The firm also participated in an international competition for the Musée Branly in Paris.

Current projects include the new theatre for the City of Saint Nazaire and three buildings for the 100 Apartments project in Paris, both due for completion in 2006. The principals regularly participate in invited competitions, most recently the Docks of Paris competition, the New Media Center (la Gaite Lyrique) in Paris and the new City Center and Casino in Knokke-Heist in Belgium.

Jakob + MacFarlane's work has been exhibited as part of both the American and French pavilions at the 2002 Biennale of Architecture in Venice, the 2004 Biennale of Architecture in Venice and the First Architecture Biennale exhibition in 2004 in Beijing.

FIRM BIOGRAPHY

JAKOB

Dominique Jakob received her degree in art history at the Université de Paris 1 (1990) before obtaining her degree in architecture from the Ecole d'Architecture Paris-Villemin (1991). She has held teaching positions at the Ecole Spéciale d'Architecture in 1998–99 and at the Ecole d'Architecture Paris-Villemin since 1994.

MACFARLANE

Brendan MacFarlane received his B.Arch degree from the Southern California Institute of Architecture (1984), and his M.Arch degree from the Harvard Graduate School of Design (1990). He has held teaching positions at the Bartlett School of Architecture in London (1996–98), and at the Ecole Spéciale d'Architecture in Paris (1998–99) and at various other schools.

PRINCIPALS

1997

Puzzle House
Theoretical project

Architectural team:
Dominique Jakob, Brendan MacFarlane

1998

T House, addition, Paris
Completion: 1998
Programme: children's loft, roof extension
Surface area: 40 m^2
Client: confidential

Consultants:
Structural engineer: Atec

Architectural team:
Dominique Jakob, Brendan MacFarlane, Vincent Chagniot

1999

Branly Museum, Museum of Early Arts, Paris
Competition 1999
Programme: museum, auditoriums, library, restoration premises, offices
Surface area: 35,000 m^2
Client: Ministry of Culture

Consultants:
Structural engineer: Setec Batiment
Façade engineer: RFR
Quantity surveyor: Bureau Michel Forgue
Acoustics: JP Lamoureux
Security systems: Casso

Architectural competition team:
Brendan MacFarlane, Dominique Jakob, Patrice Gardera, Olivier Leroy, Bruno Douliery, Alain Deswarte, Henri Rivière

2000

The Orange Box Theatre, Pont-Audemer, Normandy
Competition winner 1997, completion 2000
Programme: renovation of theatre with 300 to 600 seats (expandable)
Surface area: 1600 m^2
Client: City of Pont-Audemer

Consultants:
Services engineer: Itec
Acoustics: Cummins
Theatre systems: Deuxiéme Acte

Architectural team:
Dominique Jakob, Brendan MacFarlane, Patrice Gardera, Olivier Leroy, Bruno Douliery, Patricia Alves

2000

Maxime Gorki Theatre, Rouen, Normandy
Competition winner, completion 2004
Programme: renovation of 300-seat theatre
Surface area: 1000 m^2
Client: City of Petit-Quevilly, Seine-Maritime

Consultants:
Services engineer: Itec
Acoustics: Cummins
Theatre systems: Deuxiéme Acte

Architectural team:
Dominique Jakob, Brendan MacFarlane, Sébastien Gamelin, Laurent Gravier, Cédric Housset

2000

Restaurant Georges, Pompidou Center, Paris
Competition winner 1998, construction completed 2000
Programme: restaurant and furniture
Surface area: 900 m^2
Client: Pompidou Center/SNC Costes

Consultants:
Structural engineers: RFR; SETEC
Quantity surveyor: Forgue
Acoustics consultant: Jean-Paul Lamoureux
Security systems consultant: Casso
Lighting consultant: Isometrix

Architectural team:
Dominique Jakob, Brendan MacFarlane, Patrice Gardera, Philippe Macaigne, Olivier Leroy, Bruno Douliery, Eric Cheong

CHRONOLOGY AND PROJECT CREDITS

2001

'Books by artists', Florence Loewy bookshop, Paris
Completed in 2001
Programme: bookshop
Surface area: 70 m²
Client: Florence Loewy

Architectural team:
Dominique Jakob, Brendan MacFarlane

2002

House H, Corsica
Programme: private residence
Surface area: 500 m²
Client: confidential

Consultants:
Structural engineer: RFR
Landscape architecture: Cap Paysage

Architectural team:
Dominique Jakob, Brendan MacFarlane, Jacques Cadhilac, Gabrielle
Evangelisti, Florian Brillet

2002

A New World Peace Center, NYC, 2002
Invitation by Max Protetch Gallery: exhibition proposal for a new World
Trade Center, conceptual study

Architectural team:
Dominique Jakob, Brendan MacFarlane

2002

Renault World Communication Center, Boulogne-Billancourt
Competition winner 2000, completion 2005
Programme: exhibition halls, auditoriums, offices
Surface area: 14,000 m²
Client: Renault

Consultants:
Structural engineer: SETEC
Quantity surveyor: Bureau Michel Forgue
Acoustics: Xu
Services engineer: Inex
Façade engineer: RFR
Lighting: Isometrix
Theatre services: Cabinet Labeyrie
Security systems: Casso

Architectural team:
Dominique Jakob, Brendan MacFarlane, Patrice Gardera, Sébastien
Gamelin, Christian Lahoude, Petra Maier, Jean-Jacques Hubert, Antoine
Santiard, Oliver Page, Eric Page, Michèle Marjerus, Antoine Lacoste,
Andres Svetsuk

2003

100 Apartments, Hospital Herold site, Paris
Competition winner 2003, studies 2003–2004, completion 2006
Programme: 100 apartments
Surface area: 6000 m²
Client: RIVP/APHP city of Paris

Consultants:
Landscape architecture: Cap Paysage
Quantity surveyor: Bureau Michel Forgue
Structural engineer: Batiserf
Services engineer: Louis Choulets
Acoustics engineer: Jean-Paul Lamoureux

Architectural team:
Dominique Jakob, Brendan MacFarlane, Philippe Krych, Vincent Prunier,
Fanny Orihuela, Petra Maier, Pomine Capelier

2004

Le Fanal Theatre, Saint-Nazaire

Competition winner 2004, completion 2006
Programme: 500-seat theatre, offices, rehearsal rooms, restaurant,
bookshop
Surface area: 3500 m²
Client: City of Saint-Nazaire

Consultants:
Quantity surveyor: Bureau Michel Forgue
Structural engineer: Batiserf
Services engineer: Louis Choulet
Acoustics consultant: Jean-Paul Lamoureux

Architectural team:
Dominique Jakob, Brendan MacFarlane, Sébastien Gamelin, Petra Maier,
Atticus Manchego, Laurent Brault, Vincent Prunier, Arnaud Coutine

2006

The Docks of Paris
Competition winner 2005, currently under study
Programme: Design and fashion center
Surface area: 12,000 m²
Client: ICADE

Consultants:
Structural engineer: RFR
Service engineer: Arcoba
Landscape architect: Desvignes

Architectural team:
Dominique Jakob, Brendan MacFarlane, Patrice Gardara,
Sébastien Gamelin, Petra Maier, Atticus Manchego

Renault Communication Center, nominated for Equerre d'argent/
Le Moniteur, National Architecture Award, 2004

Excellence in Design award, *Architectural Record*, 2003

Chevaliers des Arts et des letters awarded to D Jakob and B MacFarlane
by the French Ministry of Culture, 2001

XIX Premio Compasso d'Oro for the restaurant Georges furniture/
cappellini Spa, 2001

Pont-Audemer Theatre, nominated for Equerre d'argent/Le Moniteur,
National Architecture Award, 2001

AWARDS

2004

2004 Venice Biennale, International section, September 2004

Clamour, SFMoMA, San Francisco, Autumn 2004

Architecture Biennale, Beijing, ABB, 2004

Permanent Pavillon de l'Arsenal à Paris, 100 Apartments in Paris 75019

Soft Space, Rice University, Houston, 2004

2003

Zoomorphic, Victoria & Albert Museum, London, 2003

Sign as Surface, Artists Space, New York, 2003

2002

Propositions for the redevelopment of the World Trade Center Site, Max Protetch Gallery, New York, 2002

VIII Venice Biennale, exhibited in the French and American pavilions, 2002

Biennale at Monténégro, FYR, 2002

2001

Competition model and drawings for Restaurant Georges, Center Pompidou, Musée d'Art Moderne, Paris, 2001

Paysages Hybrides, Frac Center exhibition in conjunction with the l'Institut Culturel Français of Rotterdam and Berlin, 2001

Archilab 2001, Orléans, Maison Air à Athis-Mons – model of the Florence Loewy Bookshop

La Maison du bonheur, Institut Français d'Architecture (IFA), Paris, 2001

Folds, blobs and boxes, Carnegie Mellon Museum, Pittsburgh, 2001

Maison T, Arsenal Pavilion, Venice, 2001

2000

Exhibition of the International Competition for Museum Branly, Georges Pompidou Center, Paris, 2000

Digital Real, Deutsches Architektur Museum, Frankfurt, Germany, 2000

1999

Restaurant Georges, Georges Pompidou Center, organised by *Monitor*, held at MUAR, Moscow, 1999

Archilab 1999, Orléans: Restaurant Georges, Puzzle House, T House, Maxime Gorki Theatre

Arsenal Pavilion, Paris, 1999

21 Architects of the 21st century, Buenos Aires International Biennial, 1999

1997

36 modèles pour une maison, Arc en Reeve, Bordeaux, 1997

The BART House, Bartlett School Gallery, Bartlett School of Architecture, London, 1997

1996

French Contemporary Architecture, National Institute of Fine Arts, Mexico, 1996

Books

10 x 10: 10 critics, 100 architects, Phaidon Press, 2005

Marie-Ange Brayer, Frederic Migayrou, Nanjo Fumio, *ArchiLab's Urban Experiments: Radical Architecture, Art and the City*, Thames and Hudson, 2005

FRAC Centre, *Transcapes*, 2005

Steven Skov Holt and Mara Holt Skov, *Blobjects and Beyond: The new fluidity in design*, Chronicle Books, 2005

Catalogue, Venice Biennale, 2004

Hugh Aldersey-Williams, *Zoomorphic: New Animal Architecture*, Laurence King Publishing, 2004

Marie-Ange Brayer (ed), *Architectures Experimentales: 1950–2000 – Collection du Frac Centre*, Hyx éditeur, 2003

Catalogue des collections du FRAC Centre, Hyx éditeur, 2003

Christian Girard, *Degrounding*, Casa Editrice Libria, 2004

Je veux, Onestar Press, 2003

Branko Kolarevic (ed), *Architecture in the Digital Age, Design and Manufacturing*, Taylor & Francis, 2003

Metapolis Dictionary of Advanced Architecture: City, Technology and Society in the Information Age, Actar, 2003

Joseph Rosa, *Next Generation Architecture: Fold, Blobs and Boxes*, Rizzoli New York, 2003

Catalogue, French pavilion for VII Venice biennale, 2002

Exhibition catalogue, *Identifications d'une ville au Pavillon de l'Arsenal*, Venice, 2002

Exhibition catalogue, Max Protetch Gallery, New York, 2002

International Architecture Yearbook, No. 8, The Images Publishing Group, 2002

Philip Jodidio (ed), *Architecture Now!*, Vol 2, Taschen, 2002

Temps denses 2, edition Téraèdre, In corps pore et décorpore, 2002

Catalogue, Biennale Internationale de Buenos Aires, Paysage de la Mobilité, 2001

Catalogue, *Les maisons du bonheur*, l'IFA (French Institute of Architects), 2001

Exhibition catalogue, *ArchiLab*, Air house, 2001

Philip Jodidio (ed), *Architecture Now!*, Taschen, 2001

Frédéric Migayrou and Marie-Ange Brayer (eds) *ArchiLab, Radical Experiments in Global Architecture*, Thames & Hudson, London, 2001

Joseph Rosa, *Folds, Blobs + Boxes, Architecture in the Digital Area*, Heinz Architectural Center, 2001

Peter C Schmal (ed), *Digital Real*, Birkhäuser, 2001

21 architectures du 21ème siècle, Catalogue, Biennale Internationale de Buenos Aires, 1999

Exhibition catalogue, *ArchiLab*, Orléans, France, 1999

36 Modèles pour une maison, Périphériques, Maison Mouvement, 1998

Exhibition catalogue, edited by Périphériques, Monument à La Rochelle, 1997

Periodicals

Art Press, Hors série 05, 2005, 'L'architecture contre-attaque'

Interiors, no 211, Korea, 2004

poStboks, no 05, Madrid, 2004, Florence Loewy Bookshop

A+U, no 03/2003, Japan, House H, Florence Loewy Bookshop

Atrium, March 2003, Florence Loewy Bookshop

Bauwelt, 27–28, 2003, Florence Loewy Bookshop

PUBLICATIONS

EP[s], no 1 415, November 2003, Restaurant Georges Pompidou

L'architecture d' aujourd'hui, no 346, Paris, May/June 2003, Restaurant Georges Pompidou Paris, Florence Loewy Bookshop Paris, WTC/World Peace Tower conceptual project

Quaderns, 01/2003, Spain

Techniques & Architecture, no 468, Paris, October/November 2003, 100 Apartments

Abitare, no 421, 2002, exhibition Next

AMC, no 121, 2002, Annual, Théâtre de Pont-Audemer

Architese, 04/2002, Switzerland, 'Nouveaux medias' by Judit Solt

Australian Style, no 61, 2002, 'The Future of Form' by Andrew MacKenzie

Costruire, no 32235, 2002, 'Informatica e progettazione' by Antonio Saggio

AMC, no 115, April 2001, 'Réalisation d'un Théâtre à Pont-Audemer' by Karine Dana

AMC, no 118, September 2001, 'Réhabilitation d'un théâtre Pont-Audemer'

Architectural Record, 07/2001, USA, 'Performing Arts Centers' by Claire Downey

Art4d, Thailand, 2001, Restaurant Georges

Arquitectura Viva, no 81, 2001, Ultimos Proyectos

Bauwelt, 05/2001, 'Transformation, the theatre of Pont-Audemer' by Karine Dana

Concept, no 09/2001, Korea, Process

Domus, March 2001, Italy, 'The Orange Box' by Florence Michel

L'acier pour construire, March 2001

L'acier pour construire, September 2001, Thèâtre l'Eclat, Pont-Audemer

World Architecture, no 93/2001, United Kingdom, Théatre de Pont-Audemer

A+U, no 362, 2000, Japan, Center Pompidou Restaurant

Architectural Record, 2000, USA, 'Reinventing the Pompidou Center's top-floor' by Claire Downey

Arquitectura Viva, 05/06, 2000, Spain, 'Young European Architects Amidst Planes and Folds'

Bauwelt, 2000, Museum Branly Competition

Blueprint, 12/99, 2000, UK, 'Space Odyssey' by Ray Rian

Daidalos, 06/2000, Germany, 'Smooth Takeover' by Andreas Ruby

DDN, no 81, 2000, Italy, 'Le Georges' by Brigitte Fitoussi

Frame Magazine, 03/04, 2000, The Netherlands, 'Humanising French Architecture, On the Move' by Brigitte Fitoussi

Interni, no 50, 2000, 'Georges à Beaubourg' by Brigitte Fitoussi

L'architecture Aujourd'hui, 02/2000, France, 'A interior landscape' by Laïla Belmouaz

Monitor Magazine, 2000, Project special, 'Georges' by Ana Yudina

Axis, vol 75, 1998, Japan, 'Designing Museums'

Casabella, 1998, Italy, 'Peace Monument at Vaudreuil' by Françoise Fromonot

D'architecture, September 1998, 'Il n'y a pas de petit projet' and 'Les nouveaux contextualistes' by Francis Rambert

Le Monde, 21–22 May 1998, 'Un restaurant pour l'an 2000 au Centre Georges Pompidou' by Michèle Champenois

Le Figaro, 27 April 1998, 'Des tables sur le toit de Beaubourg' by Francis Rambert

Quaderns, été 1998, Spain, 'Puzzle'

Architecture Aujourd' Hui, no 310, 1997, 'Monument à la paix' by Françoise Fromonot

Architecture New Zealand, April 1997, 'Vertical connections'

Architecture New Zealand, July 1997, 'Memory Zone'

Le Moniteur, no 4896, 1997, Visions du futur du métier de l'architecte

Le Monde, 6 July 1996, 'De mémoire de monument' by Michèle Champenois

Libération, 19 July 1996, 'Un signe de paix à Val de Reuil' by Miriam Rozen

Technique & Architecture, no 416, 1994, 'Carte Blanche à D. Jakob et B. Macfarlane'

Photography credits

Maxim Gorki Theatre: all photography by Jean Marie Montier

T House: N. Borel (1, 14, 17–19)

Branly Museum: N. Borel (4, 10, 11)

The Orange Box Theatre: all photography by Stephan Couturier

Restaurant Georges, Pompidou Centre: N. Borel (3, 33, 35, 36); Stephan Couturier (27–32, 34)

Florence Loewy Bookshop: N. Borel (1, 6, p.68–69, 9); P. Maier (7)

Renault World Communication Center: all photography by Jean Marie Montier